I Love Artists

NEW CALIFORNIA POETRY

Edited by	Robert Hass
	Calvin Bedient
	Brenda Hillman
	Forrest Gander

I Love Artists

NEW AND SELECTED POEMS

Mei-mei Berssenbrugge

University of California Press
Berkeley, Los Angeles, London

University of California Press, one of the most distinguished
university presses in the United States, enriches lives around
the world by advancing scholarship in the humanities, social
sciences, and natural sciences. Its activities are supported by the
UC Press Foundation and by philanthropic contributions from
individuals and institutions. For more information, visit
www.ucpress.edu.

University of California Press
Berkeley and Los Angeles, California

University of California Press, Ltd.
London, England

©2006 by Mei-mei Berssenbrugge

Library of Congress Cataloging-in-Publication Data

Berssenbrugge, Mei-mei.
I love artists : new and selected poems / Mei-mei Berssenbrugge.
p.   cm. — (New California poetry ; 18)
ISBN 0-520-24601-2 (alk. paper)
ISBN 0-520-24602-0 (pbk. : alk. paper)
I. Title.   II. Series.

PS3552.E77I15   2006
811'.54—dc22   2005052972

Manufactured in Canada

15   14   13   12   11   10   09   08   07   06
10   9   8   7   6   5   4   3   2   1

The paper used in this publication meets the minimum requirements of
ANSI/NISOZ39.48-1992(R 1997) (*Permanence of Paper*). ♾

Contents

I Love Artists

Aegean

Tang tang tang tang tang tang tang
ting ting ting ting ting
I eat a goat

bite into the flesh
of the spirit on the island

brown-eyed spirit flies
into emptiness
like an empty goat skull

odor of sea shell.

Perpetual Motion

1

You go to the mountains
stretch in the light aquariums
and wait—
stillness turns in its well

2

I touch your face
of rosewood and sap

the last vanished yellow
of sunset on the mountain

the first cellular light of a flank

3

Walking up the mountain
before an avalanche
you'll find the sandstone
of the peak tattooed with waves

The summit moves with the tide.

Chronicle

My great-grandfather dozed after drinking
hot liquor in his dark room full of books
When she entered to wake him without knocking
as she did every night being the first grandchild
he was dead. One fur sleeve touched the floor
Once he carried her in his big sleeve through
cold halls to the kitchen where they were burning
straw. His daughter took her smelling of wormwood
behind the fireplace to feed. It wasn't the same robe
he died in, but the same color and cloth. My mother
really can't remember the smell of lynx, herbs
against moths, nor the slowness of his step
which must have been told.

The Reservoir

1

The reservoir is trying to freeze over
with an expanding map shaped like an angel
Separated lovers on a coast keep walking
toward each other. Low sun reddens
their faces without heat

They are weary of always moving
so seldom touching, but never think
to move inland, massive and stable
Imagoes hatched on thin ice, it's
their illusion membranes are brighter
than occluded flesh of interiors

Membranes have the density
of an edge, and edges violent as lava

2

All day she walked across the tundra
He began to drive away obliquely
at exactly her speed, so she altered
her angle, aiming above him, as in a current

He departed in a zone that solidified
at his whim, so she reached for his hand
Land cracked with their weight. He seemed
to reach toward her, a hand like paper
twisted and folded over, only a surface
with wan modulations, like a map

3

Then she delicately stepped out
toward the edge, tenuous as a leaf
as if waiting for a letter
but it froze too swiftly before her
At dusk his voice broke her concentration
She turned, vexed, and saw he had not spoken.

from *The Field for Blue Corn*

3

Certain colors are the conversation
we held one dusk, that altered
from the violent afterglow of fresh bones
to the gray corolla of old ones, only minerals
As restless matrices in blue sage dissolved
a horntoad ran under a bush. I insisted it was
a baby bird. Then a baby bird *and* a horntoad
ran out. Now, on a hill I never noticed
between two close ones we've climbed, I see
at an altered angle. Some small shift in refraction
has set the whole plain trembling and hostile

4

I wondered if seasons were invented
by our brain, which is maternal, to soothe
chaotic events, since no springs here
have been alike. Moths swarmed the elm tree
one year, and bees the next, so I thought
it was the teeming, but this year is dry
austere, an anatomical drawing of the heart
taken from life, inaccurate and scientific
Branches without leaves over bare ground
pretend to reveal everything. We revolved
around ourselves as if we were central, the way
the earth was, which is not, like this plain
sun lights between the Taos Mountains and Jemez
Now, move a little to the west. Seasons are
an amulet against the heartbreak of things not unique
dulling loss by flowerings, the columbine
that died back. A rite of passage is the first
winter, we need to survive meeting strangers
as pulsating light and not explosions, the way
a flower, as "the culmination of a plant"
expresses its seductive intent

6

Color is an aspect of the light on a face
and on the pale gash of a washout in the hills
like spans of window glass on winter sky
The hue of vapors is revealed through a filter
of clouds with soulful articulation. We see
blue shadows on peaks normally glittering
with snow. I learned the palette
of diffuse days. Positive tones, finely altered
are silence and distance. In curtained rooms
a pulse beats in prisms on the floor
Other days one goes out adorned and sunburnt
All the more precious a veined wing
Undiluted brightness is an aspect with heroic
edges, in spite of common immersion in sun
as from the lover's face, veiled or aggressive
along a large but rhythmic wave. As with
land, one gets a sense of the variations
though infinite, and learns to make references

7

Please stay a little longer, at least
until the garden is turned, our old whimsical
siege on arid land, where I have seen snow peas
and columbine, even though not inert growth
Extra effort to keep a flowering vine as it is
entropy, is locked into our memory, since
we'd naively assumed flowering was natural
A sprout against its seed coat is the first
battle, after the one with air. All the seeds
seem to fall near the enemy. If I have failed
to grow herbs in a knot, as in English gardens
some motley hardy ones may take, and buckle
the topsoil with incompatible roots. Please
stay. Help me pace out the field for blue corn
If a winter has seemed to pass as only our shadows
on a rough wall, weren't they blank and rough
as apple petals blown over and over each other
to drift in heaps on the porches?

The Constellation Quilt

She stitched her story on black
silk patches from the mourning dress, quaint
as our novels will seem, but we still recognize
tonight's sky, as if there were a pattern
whose edges compose with distance, like nebulae
or namings, so triangles become Orion
Horse, Morning Star, not flanks and wings imagined
in gases, or story pieced out of intervals
from which any might grow, as if sparks ever
scatter the same, or a name assume one face
and stance, dated in cross-stitch in a corner
Stitching a name like defoliate in white thread
on white fabric leaves the leaf empty. In that
century, it was a giraffe or a bear's act. Sometimes
the only pattern seems shock waves advancing
in parallel fanned lines, leaving a tide's debris
whose pattern is moon, cryptic as if there were none
the one safe assumption. Littlest sisters eclipsed

are each another story of a marriage, using the same
scraps for different constellations, Bear, Swan
overlapping.

The Heat Bird

1

A critic objects to their "misterian" qualities
I look it up and don't find it, which must relate
to the *mystères* in religions. Stepping
across stones in the river, which covers
my sound, I startle a big bird who must circle
the meadow to gain height. There is a din
of big wings. A crow loops over and over
me. I can see many feathers gone from its wing
by sky filling in, but it's not the big bird
I walk into the meadow to find what I've already called
an eagle to myself. At first you just notice a heap
like old asphalt and white stones dumped

2

There is a curving belly. The cow's head is away from me
Its corpse is too new to smell, but as an explanation
hasn't identified my bird. Twice I'm not sure if light wings
between some bushes are not light through crow feathers
but then I really see the expansive back swoop down
and circle up to another cottonwood and light
It's a buzzard with a little red head. You say
that's good. They're not so scarce anymore. It should
have been more afraid of me

3

Fresh wind blows the other way at dawn, so
I'm free to wonder at the kind of charge such a mass
of death might put on air, which is sometimes clear
with yellow finches and butterflies. That poor heap
is all sleeping meat by design with little affect
I decide in a supermarket, whose sole *mystère* is
an evocative creak in a wheel. Not unlike a dead stinkbug
on the path, but unlike a little snake I pass over
All night I pictured its bones for a small box of mine
Today I remembered, on my last night you wanted to
linger after the concert, drinking with other couples
like a delicate dragonfly

4

And I can't predict your trauma. Potent and careless
as radiation here, which we call careless, because
we don't suspect anything. Then future form is in doubt
Like a critic I thought form was an equilibrium
which progressed by momentum from some original reduction
of fear to the horizon. But my son's thigh bones
are too long. I seduced myself. I thought
I'll give it a little fish for the unexpected. Its paw
moved. My back-bones are sparking mica on sand
now, that carried messages up and down

5

Glass that melted in the last eruption of the
Valle Grande has cooled, and you can run
among wild iris on a slope, or fireweed in the fall
Its former violence *is* the landscape, as far as
Oklahoma. Its ontogeny as a thin place scrambles
the plane's radio, repeating the pre-radio dream
At any time, they all tell us, to think of eruption
as a tardy arrival into present form, the temperate crystal
I still see brightness below as night anger, not
because of violence, but its continuousness with the past

while airy light on the plain is merciful and diffuse
that glints on radium pools. I wanted to learn how
to dance last year. I thought your daughter might teach me

6

She did a pretty good job at elucidating something
she didn't understand and had no interest in
out of duty. She has evoked a yen for dance. Any
beat with wind through it. In an apricot tree
were many large birds, and an eagle that takes off
as if tumbling before catching its lift. I thought
it was flight that rumpled the collar down like a broken neck
but then as it climbed, it resembled a man in eagle dress
whose feathers ruffle back because of firm feet
stamping the ground in wind. The other birds discreetly
passed their minutes with old drummers of stamina
but eagles entered swept ground oblivious to other drummers
making streams of rhythm in their repetitions
until pretty soon some of the other ladies' white feet
moved to them, too, bound thickly around the ankles
so their claws look especially small

7

Where I saw their fine cross-hatch was competition
not air moving through air or weather
though the water balloon she tried to dodge
as it wobbled this way and that like big buttocks
before breaking on her shoulder *was* rain. The rain
is not important. It rains, not very often
but regularly. If I am far from you isn't the current
of missed events between us an invention of potency
like a summer storm at night, or when I see you
A throw of food and household goods from the roof
to all of us became a meteor shower across fixed stars
In their parallel rain I can't judge each gift's distance

8

I looked to my right. Though sun wasn't yet behind
them, it was bright near each tree at the top
of the ridge in silhouette. These were precise
too, on a closer edge outside time, being botanical
I mix outside time and passing time, across
which suspends a net of our distance or map
in veering scale, that oils sinuous ligaments

or dissolves them into a clear liquid of disparates
that cannot be cleaned. Its water glows like wing bars
and remains red and flat in pools. On the way
to that town there were green waist-high meters on the plain
There was a sharp, yellow line on the blacktop
In rain it remains sharp, but its dimension below the road
softens and lengthens through aquifers. The eagles'
wingbones began to stretch open with practicing, so
luminous space in their wings showed against the sky
giving each a great delicacy in turns

9

They took me to the little town where they were
working, because I asked them to take me. To my left
was an old porch with long roof boards going away
from me, on 2 × 8 rafters perpendicular to them
and the falling-down house. Light descended
to my right. Narrow cracks between boards cast
a rain of parallel bright lines across the rafters
which seemed precise and gay in the ghost town
They were outside its time, though with each change in sun
they changed a little in angle and length, systematically
They were outside the carnage of my collaborative seductions
When I touch your skin or hear singers in the dark, I get

so electric, it must be my whole absence pushing
I think, which might finally flow through proper canyons
leaving the big floor emptied of sea, empty again
where there used to be no lights after dark

10

Prosaic magpies arrive about the time ribs begin
to show a beautiful scaffolding over its volume
where the organs were. The buzzard now brings to mind
a defunct windmill with a wheel hub, but no blades. The eagle's
descending back still bears, after enough time has passed
when the event is articulate, and I know its configuration
is not mixed, or our mingling, or the "intent" of a dance
If a bright clearing will form suddenly, we will
already know of it

Tan Tien

As usual, the first gate was modest. It is dilapidated. She can't tell
which bridge crossed the moat, which all cross sand now, disordered with footsteps.
It's a precise overlay of circles on squares, but she has trouble locating
the main avenue and retraces her steps in intense heat for the correct entrance,
which was intentionally blurred, the way a round arch can give onto a red wall,
far enough in back of the arch for sun to light.

If being by yourself separates from your symmetry, which is
the axis of your spine in the concrete sense, but becomes a suspension
in your spine like a layer of sand under the paving stones of a courtyard
or on a plain, you have to humbly seek out a person who can listen to you,
on a street crowded with bicycles at night, their bells ringing.

And any stick or straight line you hold can be your spine,
like a map she is following in French of Tan Tien. She wants space to fall
to each side of her like traction, not weight dispersed within a mirror. At any time,
an echo of what she says will multiply against the walls in balanced,
dizzying jumps like a gyroscope in the heat, but she is alone.

Later, she would remember herself as a carved figure and its shadow on a blank board,
but she is her balancing stick, and the ground to each side of her is its length,
disordered once by an armored car, and once by an urn of flowers at a crossing.
The stick isn't really the temple's bisection around her, like solstice or ancestor.
This Tang Dynasty peach tree would be a parallel levitation in the spine
of the person recording it.

Slowly the hall looms up. The red stair's outline gives way to its duration
as it extends and rises at a low angle.
In comparison to the family, the individual hardly counts, but they all
wait for her at a teahouse inside the wall.
First the gold knob, then blue tiers rise above the highest step,
the same color as the sky.

When one person came to gain its confidence,
she imagines he felt symmetry as flight after his fast among seven meteorites
in the dark. He really felt like a globe revolving within a globe.
Even the most singular or indivisible particle or heavenly sphere will adjust
when the axis extending beyond itself is pushed, or the sphere it is within
is pushed. What she thought was her balance flattens into a stylized dragon
on the marble paving stones.

Yet she's reluctant to leave the compound. Only the emperor
could walk its center line. Now, anyone can imagine how it felt
to bring heaven news. She is trying to remember this in Hong Kong
as the tram pulls suddenly above skyscrapers and the harbor
and she flattens against her seat, like a reversal occurring in the poles,
or what she meant by, no one can imagine how.

Chinese Space

First there is the gate from the street, then some flowers inside the wall,
then the inner, roofed gate. It is a very plain wall, without expressionistic means,
such as contrasting light on paving stones inside the courtyard to the calligraphed foundation stones.
My grandfather called this the facade or Baroque experience, rendering a courtyard transparent.
The eye expecting to confront static space experiences a lavish range of optical events,
such as crickets in Ming jars, their syncopation like the right, then left, then right progress
into the house, an experience that cannot be sustained in consciousness, because
your movement itself binds passing time, more than entering directs it.

A red door lies on a golden mirror with the fascinating solidity and peacefulness of the pond
in the courtyard, a featureless space of infinite depth where neither unwanted spirits nor light
could enter directly from outside. It lies within the equally whole space of the yard
the way we surrounded our individuals, surrounded by a house we could not wholly
retain in memory. Walking from the inner gate across a bridge which crossed four ways
over the carp moat, turning right before the ice rink, we pass roses imported from Boston,
and enter the main courtyard, an open structure like a ruin. This is not remembering,
but thinking its presence around eccentric details such as a blue and white urn turned up to dry,
although certain brightnesses contain space, the way white slipcovered chairs with blue seams contain it.

The potential of becoming great of the space is proportional to its distance away from us,
a negative perspective, the way the far corner of the pond becomes a corner again as we approach
on the diagonal, which had been a vanishing point. The grandmother poses beside rose bushes.
That is to say, a weary, perplexing quality of the rough wall behind her gives a power of tolerance
beyond the margins of the photograph. Space without expansion, compactness without restriction
make peculiar and intense account of the separable person from her place in time,
though many families live in the partitioned house now. The reflecting surface of the pond
should theoretically manifest too many beings to claim her particular status in the space,
such as a tiger skin in space.

After the house was electrically wired in the thirties, he installed a ticker-tape machine connected
to the American Stock Exchange. Any existence occupies time, he would say in the Chinese version,
reading stock quotations and meaning the simplicity of the courtyard into a lavish biosphere,
elevating the fact of its placement to one of our occupation of it, including the macaw speaking Chinese,
stones representing infinity in the garden. This is how the world appears when the person
becomes sufficient, i.e., like home, an alternation of fatigue and relief in the flexible shade of date trees,
making the house part of a channel in space, which had been interior, with mundane fixtures
as on elevator doors in a hotel, a standing ashtray that is black and white.
The family poses in front of the hotel, both self-knowing and knowing others at the same time.
This is so, because human memory as a part of unfinished nature is provided
for the experience of your unfinished existence.

Texas

I used the table as a reference and just did things from there
in register, to play a form of feeling out to the end, which is
an air of truth living objects and persons you use take on,
when you set them together in a certain order, conferring privilege
on the individual, who will tend to dissolve if his visual presence
is maintained, into a sensation of meaning, going off by itself.
First the table *is* the table. In blue light
or in electric light, it has no pathos. Then light separates
from the human content, a violet-colored net or immaterial haze, echoing
the violet ice plant on the windowsill, where he is the trace of a desire.

Such emotions are interruptions in landscape and in logic
brought on by a longing for direct experience, as if her memory of experience
were the trace of herself. Especially now, when things have been flying apart in all directions,
she will consider the hotel lobby the inert state of a form. It is the location
of her appointment. And gray enamel elevator doors are the relational state,
space behind them being a ground of water or the figure of water. Now,
she turns her camera on them to change her thinking about them into a thought

in Mexico, as the horizon when you are moving can oppose the horizon inside
the elevator via a blue Cadillac into a long tracking shot. You linger
over your hand at the table. The light becomes a gold wing on the table. She sees
it opening, with an environment inside that is plastic and infinite,
but is a style that has got the future wrong.

Recitative

Her voice on the telephone, while she is out of town performing the activities she is describing,
but with a poignant elevation of mood, is quantifiably precise, insistently formal,
as stripped down as a Palladian animation of form. Her beauty is identified with order,
liveliness, serenity, a courtly arrangement of platforms or painted stars.
Half their conversation is in shadow, so they speak in and out of a diagonal wedge of light.
The possibility of static or a gap on a starry electric night gives the impression of her body
constantly engaged in transition, but she desires to enter a body of material by talking.

In Sumer and in Egypt in the 3rd millennium B.C., speech was spoken like an arrangement of stars,
an orderly procession of luminous beings, who counted poetry with sound,
until speaking gave way to a duration that would not reconstitute, so she may appear
as a large masklike close-up and as an immobile figure in white on the bed,
who actually absorbs space.

One can paint stars on a black lead background,
equivocal stars casting carpets of desire here and there in the middle of an errand,
which up to then had proceeded in the state of non-imploring urgency of a body in diagonal,
an image of outreach or hailing. For me, it seemed love was a spiritual exercise in physical form,
and the diagonal was glints off an inferred line of sun lingering, as spring

synchronized with the double space of her desire and her desire for their presence
to be hieratic, not wholly expressive, a standard of grace in the corridor of a day,
with narcissus. If it is through counting that speech is connected to time,
then crossing an inferred estuary of this conversation is a rest in music.

Alakanak Break-Up

I

To find out the temperature, she tosses a cup of water into the air,
because it will evaporate before it hits the ground.
She goes outside and tosses a cup of alcohol into the air,
and then she keeps looking into the air.

When her attention is discontinuous, this no longer means that she
is inattentive. In the same way, they can measure the plain, now,
although plain and temperature are vacuums her heat sweeps
across, even before she has turned.

When she turns, the ice she had been standing on is changing into
foam and is about to drift away. It rumbles as it is changing.
She watches it recede, until it is a slit of light entering the brain,
because the brain is protecting itself against the light.

Here is the event horizon. You can focus on a cone-shaped rock
in the bay. You can make it larger and closer than the ice
surrounding it, because you have the power to coax the target.
This breaks up your settlement in a stretch of infinity.

Then you tie some string to a stick and toss it in front of you,
as you are watching the rock. Then you keep drawing it back.
Sometimes the stick disappears in front of you, until you draw
it back. At these times the rock has become yourself,

wearing soft bedclothes and with burned eyes.
You balance three horizons. In the same way you press down
on her shoulders and gently push the person into the ground,
which is constantly changing in the current and on the tide.

This is where they have concentrated you. All that time
you had been noting the direction of snowdrifts and stalks bent
in the south wind. Nevertheless, a storm can distract your attention.
Your attention becomes the rasping noise of a stick drawn across
the edge of a bowl at a party. It draws attention tenuously
from your fingers, the way your body starts to hurry in the wind.

This is where they have concentrated you, in order to be afraid
or in order to re-create the line between your mind and your mind
on the other side of a blue crack in the ice, so you can sit
facing each other, like ice floes folded up and cut up
and piled up against each other, and so you know enough to stop
as soon as you lose your direction.

Then, if you are on the ocean, with poor visibility, with no wind,
and you cannot be seen, please go around the outside of an ice
floe, because the ocean has dust particles, which will sparkle
and indicate the direction of the sun, she says.

When you look up, you see a heavy frost has formed on the window,
which had been damp for a while each morning, and then would dry
up and crackle. You pass the window. Ice begins to melt and drops
of water travel down the window diagonally, because of your speed.

You take the window and place it in your mouth, and meanwhile
fish line attached to a red bandanna jiggles in the dark,
because you are losing consciousness. It swarms around the rag
when you look up at it against the sky.

The dashes you had applied so carefully, in order to record rotation
in the sky have been washed away, leaving milky traces of themselves
and of their trails, so your poor map is now a circuit of spirals you
can only decode into chrysanthemums on a sleeve moving past cirrus clouds.

You are a blur of speed concentrating on heading in one direction.
It is the bank above you standing still, because you are being
held back. Sometimes in your path you see darkness that looks
like smoke. When you come to the edge of it, you realize you are
already veering away from it. You have to concentrate on the
dotted line of your lane, which is foretold in threes by the light
and ticks like a meter from your looking at them.

Sitting up, you think someone has been splashing water on your clothes.
Picking up a dash, which becomes a warm beam in your hand,
you arrange them on a board, oblivious to the sky, because
you conceive of yourself now, moving on the board or behind the board.
A square of the board lights up and becomes the single headlight
of a car, indicating another person.

If the gravity of this moment outweighs your knowledge of where
you are, that is pathetic. That is what makes the space above the
ocean so attractive, but you still know enough to travel in a
straight line through a patch of fog, and continue to walk when
you emerge, with some fog clinging to you, up to your waist.

Each time you forge an off-shoot of the river, you are hoping it
is the river. It is a little mild time. You see a row
of gulls lined up on the ice, their chests puffed toward the sun
which is the color of apricots on snow.

You pass a man lying on the snow, moving his head up and down
and singing. At first the monotony of his movement makes it hard
to concentrate on what he is saying. The snow around him has
frozen into patterns of wavy lines, so there are luminous blue
shadows all around you. This is obviously an instrument for his
location which her voice occupies. It grates across
pointed places in the form of vapor trails.

It is so mild, you are beginning to confuse your destination with your location. Your location is all the planes of the animal reconstituting itself in front of you.

2

Anyone who is all right would not be coming in covered with fog.

It is a pattern when it is moving. When it is moving collisions of things that happen produce a wavering but recognizable image that merges into the ground when it is still. It is a black diamond that condenses you mentally as it collapses. It is a black diamond on the ground, and the diamond is moving. Then it disappears when you look at it, yourself having no coincidence.

The ground is covered with ice.

Many holes in the ice are glowing with light.
You could say one light is a slanting plank that interrupts the ice. It could be a bridge, except where new ice is closing it off into a small enclosure like a holding pen or a bed. The human shines through from behind and below seams and holes in the ice. The human hovers like a mood. On a molecular level, the human remains, as a delicate glittering accent on the dateline, like a light flashing upriver, which can only be seen by the first person who looks on it, because her looking is equivalent to clocking its velocity in a chute or a tunnel to her.

She considers these the unconscious lessons of a dominant force
that is being born, and as it becomes, its being is received structure.
First ice crystals, then heavier glass obscures the light,
so she walks back and forth talking to herself, in a white soundless
sphere past the trash of the village.

She crosses pressure ridges that form a fringe between old ice
and open water. And the ice responds to her haphazardous movement.
Snow is moving about the ice, some of it settling, some of it blowing.
She notices certain portions are ice, while others are covered with snow,
which is easy to make tracks on. And she is careful not to step on the snow.

Twenty miles of frozen ridges buckle with snow,
but when she travels under the ice, the ice would be like fog.
Inside the fog, there is a jail fire. Flames lure a quantity
of what is going to happen to her into equivocalness,
by softening her body with heat, as if the house she is in
suddenly rises, because people still want her.

She prefers to lie down like a river, when it is frozen in the valley,
and lie still, but bright lines go back and forth
from her mouth, as she vomits out salt water.
This is the breakthrough in plane. The plane itself is silent.
Above and behind the plain lies the frozen delta. Above and in
front of her, fog sinks into the horizon, with silence as a material.

So, she is walking among formations of rock. Once again, she can make
a rock in a distant wash move closer to her, where it splays out
like contents its occurrence there. Once again, her solitariness
can flow into the present moment, although she seems to know what
is going to happen.

This is an image represented by a line of ice slabs facing a line
of rocks. One rock seems a little heavier and darker than the others,
but for now, they are two lines of tinkling unaccompanied voices.

The rest can be correspondingly inferred, as a line of rocks
leading toward a distant mountain, as into a distorting mirror,
which once again grows darker and denser, crossing over into mass
for a while, before returning to the little saxophone repetition
with which it began, like rubble under her feet.

Still, anything can still happen. She is still unable to distinguish
one wave from another. This is her nervous system attempting
to maintain its sweep across the plain.
Everything is still moving, and everything is still one texture,
altered from sheer space to the texture of a wall.

The route-through tightens around the nervous system, like a musculature.
It floats like a black mountain against the night sky, although she will remember
a mountain glimmering with ore. Then it darkens for her return.
The river branches and the sea has become blank as mirrors each
branch of the river flows into.

3

Sometimes I think my spirit is resting in the darkness of my stomach.
The snow becomes light at the end of the winter. The summer
is an interruption of intervals that disappear, like his little dance
before the main dances, a veridical drug.

A wafer of space beneath the ice starts to descend, like
the edge of her sleeve across a camera lens. Pretty soon
the ice will be all broken up. There is no space left. You look
down on a break-up of little clouds over the plain, as if the house
you are in suddenly rises, to relieve the nervous pressure of light.

Twenty miles of frozen ridges become a lace of moss
and puddles too flat to see and which are breathing. Here is
a snowdrift that has begun to melt. Here is an old woman
talking about a young person who is androgynous, across a distortion
of radio waves, trying to locate you. She is only moving
from her knees down.

The snow becomes light at the end of winter. How ice changes
on either side of the boat is not a tactic. The drum is a boat.
The mail route is a line of controlled electric light.
They will scatter their clothes anywhere in this light. You leave
your shirt near the snowmobile. It is initial color on the tundra.

Fog

1

Hundreds of millions of years ago, days were many hours shorter.

All things, sounds, stories and beings were related, and this complexity was more obvious. It was not simplified by ideas of relationship in one person's mind.

Paths of energy were forced to stay in the present moment by being free of reference, making it impossible to focus on two things at once, and showing by its quietness that energy of attention is as much a source of value and of turbulence as energy of emotion.

As lava burst from the ground to cover the planet, it also freed water, which escaped as massive billowing fog, a contradicting ambition of consciousness to acquire impressions and retain strong feeling.

Fog is a kind of grounded cloud composed like any cloud of tiny drops of water or of ice crystals, forming an ice fog.

Since water is 800 times denser than air, investigators were long puzzled as to why fogs did not quickly disappear through fallout of water particles to the ground.

It turns out that the drops do fall, but in fog creating conditions, they are buoyed up by rising currents, or they are continually replaced by new drops condensing from water vapor in the air.

Their realism is enhanced by smoothing away or ignoring discontinuities in the fog, for images of what we really see when we travel. Beautiful, unrepeatable, fleeting impressions can be framed only within the contradicting ambition of her consciousness to acquire impressions and to retain her feeling, a way of repeating a dream.

Large areas of the sky change from totally transparent to nearly opaque within a few minutes, although throughout a lifetime, the night sky appears remarkably constant.

Showing what they are without revealing what they are, paths of energy are transformed at the moment before their dissemination into an empty field, like dew you see on a spiderweb when the sun hits it, after there were spiders.

2

There is a great wall in the fog and rain.

There are some mountains in the mist.

There is the line of a wall in the mist. I go in and out of the fog on the rim trail, and the mountains rise in fog among yellow leaves.

There is a veil of fog between her and a sunlit flank of yellow leaves.

Slow-whirling galaxies allow stars and gas to fall into hot disks of matter, orbiting around massive holes at the centers of the galaxies, allowing a branch to spring up at the moment when snow melts from it.

Your concentration is interrupted by a shadow on the periphery of your memory of her.

Your concentration is a large array, where debris in the mind appears as an intense shower of heat radiation, like a cluster of instincts to the body.

3

As far as the transparency or relative compression of her boundaries is concerned, and your backward focus to it:

A white glass of water is hard to conceive of, because we cannot depict how the same thing would be white and clear, and how this would look. She doesn't know what description these words demand of her, since she is alone.

She can sometimes see the events of a story as if they lay behind a screen, and it were transparent, rather like a sheet of glass, since human beings can be reflected on a smooth white surface in such a way that their reflections seem to lie behind the surface, and in a sense are seen through it.

4

She can describe for you the phenomenon of feeling her way through the fog. For whom does she describe this?

What ignorance can her description eliminate?

Which person is supposed to understand her description, people who have been lost in fog before, or people who have lived on the desert and never seen what she would describe?

You try to connect the experience of being lost with something external or physical, but we are really connecting what is experienced with what is experienced.

So, when she tries to talk about the appearance of the people's feelings around her, she wants to connect how it appears to her with what is solid around her, but

she can connect appearance with how people *seem* to feel, and their communicating with each other within this appearance, from one person to another.

Is it possible for four different people in this way to have four different spatial concepts within the crowd? Somewhat different ones? Different with respect to one or another feature or heat inside a building, such as arm span or eye contact, and that could impair their mutual understanding to a greater or lesser degree? But often, hardly at all, like ice broken up on the sea.

From above, I can't tell what distance away it is.

5

It has no shape or color that is stable, as if I had fallen asleep and a long bridge appeared, where my relatives are like companions crossing a bridge.

Her friends and family are like people you meet at the marketplace.

When you look at your husband, you think of a floating flag of the roof.

Even though he is your husband, he is not stable. Anyone believes what anyone says about you.

This is a realm or field in which other people exist in subtler forms than the body in daylight. A part of the person can become visible at a time, or parts of the people, and other parts rest in folds of the fog, as if they were muffled sounds.

It would be hard for you to believe that anything within the cloud exists.

His body, which you do not see exists, having dissolved its cells into a body of a cloud, which shifts in and out of focus.

It would not decay.

The body is the space of the point of a moment in your seeing him or hearing him.

You can calm yourself by moving toward one of these points, the way you move along your own breath.

6

You could try to make some fog into a piece of white cloth. This is impossible. Though it is visible, it is not a concrete substance. She tried to make a delicate cloud into a cloth. She could not, so that is why he is staying here.

Or she could try to alternate dissolving in the light with dissolving in the dark, for speed.

At night, she could see as if the country were illuminated, as if it were day. She could see each person's face clearly, and she could remember if she had ever known this person before.

Dreams cannot disturb the fog or you, because your environment has no territory. There is no territory in a fog environment.

7

Lack of clarity within your environment is tormenting. It is felt as shameful. We feel we do not know how to even out a place for ourselves, where we should know our way about. But we get along very well inside buildings, without these distinctions, and without knowing our way about the decrepit structures.

In any serious interaction between them, not knowing your way about extends to the essence of what is between them. What can appear emotional is caused by the emission of energy out of her body, which you feel, but there is also such a thing as "feeling something as luminous,"

thinking of him as the color of polished silver or nickel, or a scratch in these metals.

8

This fog in space and light and dark is analogous to the solid ice of a very pure environment, and how it cracks and gets water from one stage to another.

Its area of wide space varies in lightness from place to place, but does it look foggy to her in the darker places? The shadow that a cloud casts is in part darker. She sees the parts of the space that are farther away from the light as darker, but still white, even though she would have to add black to depict it.

Looking around in her room or any wide space in the evening, she can hardly distinguish among the people around her, and now becomes physically frightened of them.

And now, illuminate the space and describe each one you saw in the mist.

There are pictures of dreams in rooms in semi-darkness, but how can she compare the people in these pictures with those she saw in semi-darkness?

9

The bright light slows the senses. A picture of the space in bright light, as if etched by a laser, can slow your sense.

When we see or experience something with the senses, and the senses get slowed, we can stop at this object, for example, a person who is beautiful.

As soon as we see this person, perception is blocked by the desire to go toward the person, with the misunderstanding of fog as thought that just runs on and on. Her awareness is completely lost in distracting clearings of space.

10

The sky, which illuminates everything we see, can be gray. This can be true of someone around you in your family. How can she tell merely by its or his appearance that gray isn't itself luminous?

Thinking of him as the color of polished silver or other metal.

The fog of the way we feel our way into this focus, seeking by feeling, lies in the indefiniteness of the concept of continuing focus, or distance and closeness, that is, of our methods of comparing densities between human beings.

Is foggy that which conceals forms? And does fogginess conceal forms, because it obliterates light and shadow, the way light obliterates or shadow obliterates, also?

Black does, but fog doesn't necessarily take away the luminosity of a color.

Darkness is not called a color.

The first solution which occurs to us for the problem of the appearance of another person is that ideas of actual feeling instead of the appearance of feeling refer to points of tiny intervals or patches in the other person.

How are we to compare the feelings between two such intervals, simply by letting one's memory move from one to the other? If you do this to me, if you remember me, how do we know this feeling has not changed in the process? If you do remember correctly, how can we compare the feeling without being influenced by what has happened since,

the way we call a complex of intervals with which you depict the family member, his emotion with respect to you, as if the person were a piece of rose-colored glass?

Would he have the same emotion in a crowd as a piece of rose-colored paper?

A story line develops based on your moving from one breath to another, and you start to want to continue it, like a span of good health or exceptional beauty. You want to continue it forever, and your memory gets involved, in how you perceive the space around you and the human beings or descendents in the space.

You will eventually feel so empty inside, among your family and in your memory of your family, that even while you continue breathing, your breath will not bring volume or space into your lungs.

They counted her more accurate and more inaccurate memories as black and white stones.

The more accurate memories turned out to be white on the outside, but they were unconditioned by the desire to form story out of her memory, continuing story, the way we wish this space and light to continue.

Therefore, we appreciate fog, as the power to make the space continue beyond a single perception into raw material or youth of the body, like a body of light.

It dissolves now at the top of her head, now five lights into her heart. Now, it dissolves into her body. Her friends dissolve into light. They dissolve into her family, which seems to dissolve into clouds that were already full of light.

It is not so much the quality or brightness of light, or her understanding of this light, as the number of times she dissolves. The faster she can dissolve into the space, the better.

It is almost as if the complete dark would be ideal.

Empathy

1

For me, the insignificant or everyday gesture constructs a choreography of parts and what touches me is where the inarticulate, the error or tension, finds concrete manifestation and is recognized. —Beverly Dahlen

First, I see roses in the dark with him, a compaction of spare light,
then a road through the woods in pitch dark. How she perceives the corridor in the dark
is a space within the time in which they were moving,
as if perspective of a space in the dark constructed a hierarchy in her mind,
in reverse of how the contents of her wishes remain unchanged and timeless,
so the innermost nature of her wishes is as much known and unknown to them as the reality of the
      external world.
It is as incompletely presented by what she can see as is the external world
by communication with someone she wishes for.

In this way her interrogation of him appears instead as a dialogue pertaining to uses of power,
because she can only remember what has been consciously said to her,
so that her feeling of identifying with him is like a quick flash or a signal.
When it is intense, tormenting and continuous, it's using itself to construct a rhetorical story again.

This state of confusion is never made comprehensible by being given a plot,
in the same way a complicated plot is only further complicated by being simplified,
although connectedness may not always be an artifice,
for example, when it reveals ways in which she construes what she perceives
according to an internal connection which will announce its conflict in the plot,
a tension like his mistaken gesture, interesting as a site of power formation.
It may well be where the feeling of mysteriousness occurs
in which she believes him, but she doesn't want to prove it,
because an appearance in the dark will not deceive after enough appearances
and everywhere, sooner or later, there will be a hint of a tree or space above a lake,
so describing something as it is could by precise reference gain a neutral tone,
but in this case adheres to his and her manner of asking
where is the space, instead of what space it is.
There occurs an interval of northern lights over their walk, whose circumference is inferrable,
but whose outermost region lacks any known form of registration,
such as before that and before that.

2

In an empty stadium they alternate the refrain of a song in Japanese. The light is harsh
on rows of seats like cells of a honeycomb under high magnification.
The entire stadium resembles a honeycomb or geodesic dome turned inside out and concave.
He is saying, I am here. She is saying, where are you.

Speech and thought arise simultaneously as hysterical question. An idea is a wish.
As a descriptive stream or spontaneous reaction to him,
speech serves as a starting point for uncovering a story through translation from wish into desire,
but when thought becomes reflective, a problem of interpretation enters the stream of emotion itself.
The speaking becomes fixed, although there is no such thing as repetition.

The speaking is a constant notation of parallel streams of thought and observations,
whose substance is being questioned in a kind of oral thought at once open and precise,
but with a tension between ideas and her sense of scandal at invoking a real person.
He makes a rift or glimpse, both generative and relative to the glimpse,
a liberty of interruption, or exclusion, inside the stadium
in light so bright she sees her eyelash as a golden line reflecting on the inside of her sunglasses.
In the same way the song must never be allowed to threaten the presentation of what takes place in the song,
so that she may try to develop empathy for what she really wants to happen to her,
instead of desire being the song.

3

Anything with limits can be imagined, correctly or incorrectly, as an object,
even some language in the way that it is remembered, if you consider
each repetition a fact or object of varying strength in various situations of frequency and quantity,
and although you can never vary an unconscious wish,

which can only reveal itself in the contingency of the words, sexualizing the words,
the way a shadow moves up a wall of trees growing intensely gold at sunset.
Her equivalent is a time-lapse photograph of lightning, in proportion
to each moment you are looking. It is her attempt to show him a lightning storm
or any interval of colored light on the plain as what is good in life, the person, and what is good,
so instead of saying what time it is, she is asking, where is the time, its ratio as an open lens
on clear sky. It may be relevant to ask if this kind of autobiography limits formal
or object possibilities, meaning less neutral or less real within her empathy for what is good in life
from his point of view. For her, feminizing an art of presence
such as moving or speaking, with its distinct kind of maneuverability,
is akin to those collages that verge on trompe l'oeil. Only when she looks closely
does she realize that that head is really not the one connected to that body,
although everyday gestures or tensions accrete an intimacy she can recognize.
Be that as it may, real and constant luminosity of the parts can create
a real self who will remain forever in the emotion of a necessary or real person.
To deny this is to deny the struggle to make certain meanings stick.

The Swan

He calls it their stage, which echoes our first misrecognition of unity. Instances
of false unity, he calls the imaginary, and he locates in them sites of her dreams,
out of which she is able to want him. The way stage lighting can be a story by itself, now
she makes time for a story, not coming from her or her coming from her story, but both from before,
seeing a flock of birds fly up from a frozen pond, while you stand in the wind, instead
of hearing wind about to arrive across a huge space, so that her train passes a lagoon
in Connecticut, *and* she sees swans swimming at the edge of ice piled against the shore, feminine swans.
Remembering what I heard you say and fixing my desire for you simultaneously, a meaning
of instability, not hesitance, holds you *and* the swans accountable for making the desire,
although the meaning of the desire existed prior to being desired.

Truth effects produced within a dream, neither true nor false in themselves,
operate through repetition to convey an illusion of truth or meaning,
which may be the constant sum of varying systems of dreams, like birds startling from a cottonwood tree
and wind about to arrive, or your seemingly high standards for truth, considering that
where femininity is concerned, similar effects yield various meanings, as when a woman photographed
on two separate occasions on the street at random by a famous photographer, who's dead now,
still finds herself in a purely theoretical relationship with herself in relation to him,
which he refuses to merge with the intermediacy of real light. That immaterial matter truly
leaves objects their own places, lighting and illuminating them. Therefore,

she pays attention to absurd and trivial details where her desire dissolved, among
all sorts of things that happened, both in the present and in general, so her focus on absurdity appears
to be a spontaneous part of the desire itself, where coincidence and nonsense merge in a lover,
until the sky would look on you as a composite of video monitors on surfaces slowly disintegrating
into ice swans which resemble, for example, an opera house.

Finally, one must sort of drop one's reserve, which could be a kind of definition
of physical beauty, without which no transformation takes place, such as
if you were a mother, the interval between the child and you. This is analogous
to her own physical beauty. It dominates, but does not determine its own content
or its experience, because the dream was not a concept but a means of generating experience,
so that the mother and I desire, but the child *is* a desire, in spite of the child being physical.

A flock of birds flying up acquires the shape of her arcs across the ice, a mirror stage
echoing our first misrecognition or the imaginary, to look again and then look,
so if he says or she says, my dream about you is older than my knowing you,
does that mean it was dreamed before your meeting him or her?
The meaning of the dream existed prior to the dream, and then I met you and then I dreamt about you,
gratifying an enigma that was solved and then posed, with a resulting fullness
in the dreamer, as with a child to replace himself or herself, or as verisimilitude onstage.
Its story is light that moves from cue to cue as over ground.
It resembles an arm reaching out to defend you at a sudden stop, but is rhetorical,
the way your arms full of white down inscribe an immense volume above the ice.

Forms of Politeness

I

Taking advantage of the relationships and interaction, which actually exist between what happens
to her and her desire, she creates some metaphors both obvious and opaque, as screens of rays crisscrossing
the landscape in which herself and what she expected from you in the way of support coincide,
so that I and you resemble each other, now. The way they light the land like infrared without a trace
on film, really, part of your image was linked so closely to my desire, it remained inside my body.
It never reached the emotions, which tend to damage the body, but which memory requires.
Thus a formal device was discovered for detailing information that was intimate and largely unacceptable
to what I thought I required from you, regarding beauty in idea and form. She expected distress
to automatically bring about this beauty, like a woman's theft of fire rope from your house,
but not her hanging in the orchard by the house. She was a stranger to you.
She was never in your consciousness. Hence she was never forgotten.
She is in you the way direct experience generates consciousness, adding the energy of its materialization.

To live another person's biography is not the same as to live his or her life.
She constructs a story line or cluster of anecdotal details, like clothes around the body,
instruments of both defense and expansion, which give meaning to fluctuations, such as in pleasures

occurring between herself and you. Her sunglasses swathed in feathers express
the contingency of a light and a space, so that the anecdote of a hanging could be utilized
as colorist or combinatory data, instead of her instinct for the imaginary in which what she imagines
represents what happens, whether or not it misrepresents it.

Sometimes it happens during a routine she represents by evenness of light on the land
or when things usually mean nothing, like harmony in light, what happens and something to mean
join accidentally. The thing isn't what it is, but it is like what it is.
Like a fake, it doesn't mean anything, although there is something to mean,
so that her solitude is the guise of unending repetition of a hanging or her relationship with you,
in which all that is to be included will find a place. This is empathy or sharing her intuition with her.
You look into someone's eyes as if you were seeing through the face.

2

Because it's not possible to absorb more than one insight at a time,
there seems to be a contradiction between the visual or space, and the context or meaning.
She felt deep uneasiness with the image of this sunset of unnatural energy, its sinister expression
of an order of impossible beauty we thought we lost, accounting for the intensity of yellow light on the hill,
which is not a thing, *and* it is not a metaphor, the way your life is not a metaphor to her, or
the way intense light on the hill is a recollection *en plein air,* in the sense that it happened.
Soon the background turns gray and the hill regains its natural color, but there are three dimensions of gray.
This is a metaphor for the fact that the hanged woman actually made contact with you, although you
    never knew her.

There is a link with her appearance, as with sex, or the way a name is attached to something
after naming it, by the occurrence of its name, in this case linking with the appearances
or biographies of a whole parade of lovers, so what she thinks of as human help from him
is no longer dependent on changing her desire for him in the present, but is a substitute for it.
The landscape is empty *and* it is immanent. The context of the woman in its reality
may differ from the context in which the viewer thinks about her, the element of transparency.
The way the viewer thinks about her is the way low clouds extend a landscape. The viewer
is acting on the landscape in consideration that the context of the viewer distinct from the context
of general human help could be a metaphor for itself.

There were yellow-leaved trees behind a screen of green ones at the edge of the orchard.
They are not a border between organization and decay of autumn trees, which are organized.
The yellow leaves around your feet have an impossible beauty that was achieved and then lost.
A way you can define a woman is to remember everything the woman is not.
If you move your head fast enough, you can all of a sudden discern the whole structure
of the surface of each leaf, and it links in your stomach, as with sex.
If you remember not desiring her fast enough, you can all of a sudden discern her whole body.
You can feel in your stomach the way any moment that happened and in which you think about her goes
a long way toward convincing you of the autonomy and pre-existence of her form.

3

Her concentration became a direct experience of his life, an erotic concentration.
Her biography of her persistently locates the point of impact of one's own system of representations,
insofar as vision itself is a representative operating on what she sees,

and for which a particular light can represent an initial condition. Even the slightest movement
of a hand or a finger is controlled and emphasized as by a spotlight of this sensitiveness,
the way repetition is a cessation of the potential for conscious experience, or death,
visiting the same places during the same seasons, at almost the same hour,
so that landscape could be a simple repetition, which thrives on reproduction,
in order to resolve what is happening into its own combination or name of words in the form of its time,
and in order to defer the story.

In a way, her memory is a theory about how the hanged woman looked to her in the orchard,
which she has to respect, in the sense that the landscape's immanence is an organically developing
failure of its language to speak its content. The connection between word and idea corresponding
to the landscape is retained, but the connection between the word and the landscape is lost,
so the shadow of a hill stays dark during lightning. How she sees the lightning
is a time lapse into the planar dimension, a hierarchy of grammar or deference
by way of the word belonging to her such as lady suicide or woman suicide,
because the woman doesn't die in her own absence or in effigy, so that
no existing philosophy and no philosopher will know soon, enough points with enough speed
to handle the richness of her reconstruction of her or him for long. He starts to see
patterns in the words and the patterns are pretty to him and distract him.

It is well known that lightning is attracted to body heat, a person on horseback
or a large saguaro, the way a racket of birds in the morning is a kind of empathy for two people.
If we retain the belief that her image of him or her, let's say him, is a pre-requisite for
gaining consciousness of the unknown person, we suppose there is no direct channel of communication
to the unknown person, with the result that facts about him or her must exit into the world,
before a life can be perceived between the light and dark of function or the object, and desire or the image.
At any time one can turn into its opposite, like desire or a screen, and the object
or her story and him, who does not so much convey an image as a background

to the biography. So, he says, she must emphasize references and conditions of her own life
over its memories, or what she sees of the landscape by the manner of its illumination,
unless she says it is illuminated within the arms of a great cottonwood, yellow or green,
a faith of imaginary or real connotation repeating itself from him, like alternating current
or radioactive dirt being turned up that registers on her without marking her.

4

Her persistent observation, even after the frost, is of each leaf coinciding with its luminousness,
because of its structure as a lighted space and which shows brightness in idea and form,
so you have to maintain your own consciousness in order not to be unconscious with me.
Even if we can uniquely bridge the gap between the fact of a frost and the value
of luminousness, and even though these intrinsic properties of the plant may not be what it feels.
What it feels may be a space with pillars, so with light the space extends, as in what you believe
to live with. A belief is a word-like object. You can focus your attention on it down to a point,
like desire or memory of a strong feeling. You have a certain amount of control over your feeling
about general human help by changing what you believe, which embodies the memories
your speech is empowered to represent, she says.

Space is material, but seems to open up a beyond, which is thought to defy material in its failure
to speak its content. It still cues this content by links or desires, as to a form of physical appearance.
To the extent that she can reconstruct a context or pornography in her body suitable for a hanged woman,
a contingency is beaten back, critically. In the sense that events happening at the same time are
meaningful, but not connected, there are events which mean nothing, though there is something to mean.

This is an easy way to expect with desire from moment to moment, while the woman was hanging herself,
as if consistency and the quest for certainty were not emotional,
as when a person begins telling a story, leaves move.
He believed that when a life is valuable, there is further value when it is responded to
as valuable, but this could occur through evaluative judgement, without his attendant emotion.
The product is in one case consistent manners, in the other, beautiful manners.

from *Honeymoon*

1

Though relations with oneself and with other people seem negotiated in terms secretly confirmed
by representation, her idea of the person's visibility was not susceptible to representation. No matter
how emphatically a person will control his demeanor, there will be perspectives she cannot foresee or
direct, because there is no assignable end to the depth of us to which representation can reach,
the way part of a circle can be just the memory of a depth. The surface inside its contour,
like the inside of a body, emits more feeling than its surroundings, as if
the volume or capacity of relations would only refer to something inside I can't see,
that the other person and I keep getting in the way of, or things in the landscape while they are driving,
instead of the capacity being *of* your person.

2/3

If the tree is yellow in the fall in mercury light by the river, I feel it gathering its color
from the river. An orange moon is partially hidden in the clouds in darkness. Whenever
or wherever it is possible to speak of recognition, there was a prior hiddenness or border of the circle.
It's like driving without headlights on the plain, the moon's appearance of a lake by a power plant, a dead lake,

whose color neither hides, nor doesn't hide a perspective. I call it color, if the way
the texture of skin on his hand changes in moonlight were a color, instead of a fantasy,
so that the physical idea of his privacy is not made clearer by the idea of his secrecy.
It is the same sentence as trying to explain how her assessment could not wait for her uncertainty.

You would be hiding behind a pane of glass in the atmosphere, or an example inaccessible to what
you are hiding, as if the beauty of the person, during a daydream, may flash across your mind,
like an animal across the landscape, forcing an exclamation from you, when you may not remember its name.

4

She is not the name of a person, nor *there* of a place, but they are connected with names.
There is a way of traveling by rotating an orientation, while she remains within herself.
He moves his hand across the shadow, and it tints delicate skin on the back of his hand. He
has a doll in his mind on which he can predict what she will be feeling, as if he would not
touch the doll, until her actual feeling would make contact with the object of his thought.

Why science does not use a word like *she* or *there* is why the hand cannot make a sharp edge in the sand.
The hollow his hand would make in bright sand, micaed, was the place where the wing of the person
would fold into itself, almost a shadow on skin. The fold is the object or resemblance
between the head turning over a shoulder and the wing folding.
He touches her shoulder at the place where the wing would begin, while she is sleeping.
She can concentrate on objects in the room and his talking to her, but the context is of losing herself
in possibilities like vowels, or birds during a period of plastic song, in which syllables are repeated
or rehearsed over and over. The head turns and lays itself in a hollow of skin along the ribs,
like a color laying onto the back of his hand, which could be one of her own thoughts.

6

If one string line of a bone crosses another properly, an area of brightness or intensity is created,
so that a skeleton, because it was hidden, appears to have been exposed, almost inadvertently,
in the stance of a young boy extracting a splinter from the foot resting on his knee, his hands
grasping the delicate foot. He makes a seamless extension from the space of the canyon into her mind.
Does seeking a cause make a line tremble, an act of the eye and the light, so that a space
will not stretch immovably, nor each rock place itself as individual?

This occurs on the skin of his fingertips, instead of along fissures of your thinking,
reflecting the brightness of a line, without the *idea* of the line.

8

She has to get right the occasion for visualizing his concept of the doll, but she cannot. While
she cannot experience the meaning of his assessment about the doll, it seems rags to her. So,
she has to justify her blindness to its hunger, for example. She would say, I think
she has eaten already. She would scatter crumbs on her own dress to prove this. But
this place in this light may be a place you don't know, a route you both traveled after dark
to a north rim. You have a feeling of having traveled through the space, without recognizing it.
Not recognizing the doll would have to be something you both study, like a dead language.

She thinks his relations with his own mind may flash intuitions, which force him to pass over
any attempt to say anything to himself. Not as the child would throw a ball out of its crib, and you
would carry it back. He would like to pass something over to one side that does not come back.
How you look into the canyon, a relation to lit and unlit complexities of islands on the canyon floor,
is the complicated question of looking, and the right answer that comes back. The more
complicated the question, the less light would come back, until no light comes back.
You would know everything you see in the first place, but the terms of your recognition grow
increasingly intimate and ecological, like the light of the gold of jewelry on you, which
while it is still light, is still becoming abstract.

10

A creature walks on the quiet floor of the canyon, a dry floor, sparking with mica, under which water flows,
and turns its head aside from a thorny bush with red seeds hanging down. The light is so bright
its volume would be a source to see whiteness from, which falls on a hand or on jewelry differently.
If she walked to the edge of the canyon and looked down, the creature would pass twelve feet below.
Like an image, it would absorb her interest, or like an oxygenation along the miles of the insides
of its living cells. The creature is a motive, which could generate an image of her own body
disappearing and appearing again after an interval or length of the canyon.
This occurs center stage, with footlights illuminating it, where she is the footlight.
She can trace paths through the space of a canyon, generating a motive of it which to light,
a case where there would be some way of applying the color, like some form of light projection,
saturating or fusing all the particles at all levels of the insides of the capacities.
It is how the ghost of an image was made to appear in his mind.
How deeply he feels it is not a matter of what feeling "a reason" causes in him.

11

The human being, troubled by limits, creates a trip for herself, which re-creates her
as spacious. Now, she projects expanse onto endeavors, such as the representation of an angel,
or the way the colors of the world would lay over the world, a pleasurable collation of objects,
as of hues of the shadow of an emergence place.
It passes a richness of seeing or believing back onto the impasto of the colored things,
in which anyone else may mean anyone other than the two of us, or anyone other than you,
and you will go, who are the color of a seam and not a doll
of painted bisque which makes matter protuberances or patches of invisible places across a space.
A cloud in the morning folds over a monument on the plain, a vector like an avalanche of mist concealing it.
She creates a dark flank of a mountain, a person's thoughts or feelings passing across the person,
    concealing the person.
She wonders what the body would reveal, if the cloud were transparent.
It pervades the creation of a motive, like the action of the heart.

Ideal

I did not know beforehand what would count for me as a new color. Its beauty is an analysis
of things I believe in or experience, but seems to alter events very little. The significance of a bird
flying from grapes in a store relates to the beauty of the color of the translucency of grapes.
There is a space among some objects on a table that reminded her of a person, the way the bird reminded her,
a sense of the ideal of the space she would be able to see. Beauty can look like this around objects.
A plastic bag on a bush, moving slightly, makes an alcove, a glove or mist, holding the hill.
Time can look like this. The plane of yourself separates from the plane of spaces between objects,
an ordered succession a person apprehends, in order to be reminded.

2

Two particles that make a continuum or ideal, in how the space between them relates to a third event,
as how clouds against a windowpane admit space that continues to a cloud on the mountain,
a sheath of a space of feeling in material sheaths of her body for perceived order, depend
on your having felt the relation. A horizon forms around his voice through which no sound can pass.

This voice is a feeling of remembering there was a situation in my dreams in which she would be alive.
The event could occur. A line could differ for a particle along a straight or a curved space.
He sees a relation like a new language in accidental spaces between objects, which we cannot,
as if he were seeing a color that had not existed before, and then, we can make the color.

3

You import the magenta orchid, locating this particle at a green fern, import the yellow poinciana.
It looks like the surface of the space of an analysis, but you suspect it is time, because your feeling
is changing. She makes a continuous surface among particles of table space and times of harvesting the
    elements
of a bouquet. Then one particle starts to move backward, suffusing her body, the way light gains character
suffusing berries or a cloud, by who sees it. The illusion of meaning of the third dimension, from which
his inner voice speaks is the gold of a frame. So, she cannot distinguish a house on the horizon
from a hawk lifting away, symbol acting as a word. Her sense of a sequence becomes perceptual,
like perspective on structures, putting the scale of an orchid next to human scale in designing the space.

4

I make a relation in time between the hawk hovering above her on the mountain in sun
and sun on a crow over me, turning the wings gold. I think I am tracing the nature of the color
of a feather, but I trace around a gold frame through which to examine the nature of a crow.
A wren in grapes reminding her of the woman, is how color belongs inseparably to your consciousness of her,
without being the consciousness. Gold on a wing bears the illusion of the content of a symbolic dimension.

Light on a wing, not of a crow, solves this problem of content by being an anomaly. Then
clouds lower the light. The land's planes close and grow distinct and dark-colored, making an ideal time.
A horizon retains its transparency, while you look at the relation between spaces and what he says,
as if the smallest particle of matter were a pronouncement, not a thing, so the white plastic bag becomes
a wing-like space between mist and the mountain. What is the whiteness of a reminder, becoming a
    pronouncement?

5

Here is the body of the person, his torso facing you, head and feet in profile.
There is a twist of space between the front arm and the back arm. Time goes there.
The arm that turns toward you is personal, the arm that turns away is the impersonal.
These types of flows that built the space go on building it, where you are trying to live.
She is making a line between the space inside a glove on the mountain and the moment of an orchid's
harvest, a bird's movement from a box of grapes and a bird's silhouette suffused with gold,
the scale of a bird and the scale of a man inside the event horizon of his oracle, where
heads do not look at each other, because each meaning that begins there flows into a different emotion.
This is a description of the content of the apprehended space between objects on a patio table.
In the sense of being that it is a new feeling, it is more like a coincidence of focus, where time is.
In the sense that it is a new color, it is more of an ideal than an anomaly.

Endocrinology

1

The bird watches a man and woman dance. He touches her stomach. There's circulation around her
in intercapillary space, empty or hollow, in relation to organs. A virus transfers firefly genes
to a tobacco plant. The plant glows in the dark. How much evolution derives from "something in the air,"
not a square of light above a niche in a white wall. Light, your intestines. Fluid, lines of light. As if,
when you think about something, it already has a frame that's *a priori*. Think before that moment,
    freedom is inside there.
Think before the man and woman, their freedom of an animal among silvery trees. Which trunks light
    hits is an endocrine
permutation, a state of being or a physical state. Hormones are molecules, material, invisible. Their flow
    is random,
mesh through which a body is sensed, not an image. The form of her body is important,
as how she is here, though there's no physical evidence of her physical suffering.

2

Hormones provide a mechanism by which the body relays chemical signals through cells perfused by blood.
There's a structural need to make tectonic episodes which might otherwise become pliant.
Conceiving of the body as a space of culture tends not to refer to it as nature, unless it's been taken away
    by disease,
hairy ears, genital ambiguities, like a shamanistic object, not generic. Because she's in a body, it makes
    decisions.
Black rock in a dry river, weeds tangled at the base, something heavy enmeshes with something light.
The material, of non-negotiable contingency, the feeling, a different structure on different physical levels.
A pool in the forest gleams with organic matter, its depth of the possibility of an imbalance in the body,
when luminosity detaches itself from feeling as emanation, transparency, a structural need to become
disorganized. What is physical light inside the body? A white cloth in a gold and marble tomb, to focus
    expression of the tomb.
Shortly after phagocytosing material, leukocytes increase their oxygen consumption and chemically
    produce light.
During pregnancy, the fetoplacental unit under the curve acts as a gland.
If the mother is diabetic, the fetus becomes her mother's endocrine system. This occurs in all animals
whose circulations are linked. Bone cells of an irradiated animal derive from the marrow of its parabiont.
Later, their systems associate like writing, knowing edges of a system and areas between, an outpour
of molded sand with iron rocks in crevices, as in a story she accepts not knowing if her lost child is alive.

3

The bird sings on a strawberry the size of a melon. Cells release hormones into
intracellular space, where they enter local, fenestrated capillaries.
A bird eight feet tall with disproportionately huge claws and beak.
The woman, moon-faced, hair grows from her, and she feels desire for the man touching her abdomen,
that feels like love. Prolactin in our bird induces nest building.
Estrogen induces her concept of his luminosity, detaching itself from his color. Her hands enlarge.
She can't see where her sadness ends and someone else's is.
The line between chemical and emotion is the horizon inside a niche in her body, transferring non-being
    to utility.
She lives on moisture from dew condensed on soil surfaces from night air.
The strawberry sprouts a fantail of petals. Air flames on her skin.
She believes the body, though densely saturated, is generic, dreaming the same nightmare as the child.
His presence triggers latent feeling beyond feeling for her, with enormous affection for her body.
Blood drips under a white feather of the wounded bird. A vein puts the organ in the background.
She concentrates on manipulating her organs to pull the white square of light precisely into the niche.

4

A woman leans her arms on the table, forearms abnormally long.
Her milk flows and flows. She cries and cries.
These are unaccountable imperfections in the numerical fabric, not mysteries.
A wire crosses in front of a line on a wall, while its shadow seems to cross behind it.
The place where a word originates in her body is the physical source of her sense of beauty, so you can

change the word for "happiness" that was, formerly, "innocence." The respiratory system, when
    stimulated, produces
a characteristic sighing. The thymus expends itself during stress and collapses, so an autopsy finds only a
    membrane.
Touching a wall produces the sound of touch on the other wall. Feedback between health and fate unfolds
so fast, there's no way one step in the chain can be based on the previous one.
An associative smear or aura requires her to be in a body, in order to make decisions.
Lack of cloud cover causes thermal energy on the desert to return rapidly to the sky at night.
Oxygenating molecules makes light. Lighting the organs, they turn white.
He loved her body as much as he loved her as an individual.

5

There is a space. You see something at the far edge, and your eye going over this space
makes a whole, like watery mass in a gourd, the feeling of old organs no longer crucial to or inside
    themselves,
while remembering people you loved, which flowed from the physical, about which you made decisions.
To make this whole, any object, brings into being something not in nature, an interior measurement,
yourself, not yourself, bursts of growth when you sleep. Her back bleeds. A spray
of blood on the snow. She sits on her hands physically preventing herself from scratching.
The child, her sense of the world being crucial to or inside itself, of memory and specificity, like script.
B cells grow for years in a petri dish. The sick, immortalized cells don't know to stop growing.

Where your eye goes over space to the horizon makes a whole, but where sky meets earth, the fragment is not the same as a whole. Desert ferns covered with reflecting hair may insulate the fronds. Radiations of a state barely embodied, then dissolving in counter-reflections of light.

There's an engine. He cannot separate from the loved person, to shed the loved body.

Irises

I

In a world which transcends the confines of her transient being, she can reach
and bring existences within the compass of her life, without annulling
their transcendence. These invisible entities infuse the visible with femininity,
showing their non-location by the adjectival focus of her mind. You place sixteen girls
in a meadow and always fill it. They're everyone, the world, implicit promise.
Her image of you, a transparency on her desire, is like a contact print of irises on film.
Their shallow space implies expansion within it of irises and shadows against a blue wall.
So, she proposes a soul of fine-grained material, in order to hold this promise,
like ghosts above a pond taking on heat, blurring its register over itself. Remembering
an insect would be, as if you looked into a shallow box of insects and their shadows.
If I dream I see light on a new bud in the woods, this is feeling used as thought,
beautiful because of my attempt to contain it.

2

This person is incorrigible in how things seem to her, that the body is responsible
for actions we share with brutes, for example: reflex, light reflected from a wolf
in the eyes of a sheep exciting flight. If feeling is thinking, insecurity accompanying
her flight has no parallel in a sheep. Her feeling for a fog of wild cherry in wet woods
is an appearance. Its reality is exhausted by how the fog seems. A screen of dogwood
on a ridge, like a person in front of blue mountains, can appear sinister, implicitly
shadow and breath. Her sheer imagining above the pond is like blood in a dragonfly wing,
because some blood must flow in a wing that appears to be glass. Girls fill the stage.
For a still moment, we see the world as implicit promise, something human that leaves the body
at death and goes off on its own. The more wispy the mind, as at the green edge
of a dogwood blossom, the more fit to catch sight of such an invisible entity as "parallel,"
its distinct substance capable of having all mountains thought away and still being around.

3

Sun lights a man walking out a green door and the scale of him against the door.
How sunlight fills the apple tree is how the body carries the weight of appearances to her.
When her feeling about his feeling for her goes, his appearance becomes very heavy.
Because something human will leave the body, the beauty, as of proportions between leaves
proceeding backward from the growing point of a vine, acquires its privilege from one who feels it,
not beauty's actual transparency. The transparency of a leaf against the size it will attain
along any vector of the stem, like iris shadows on a wall, has the fluidity of a veil, not opaque
size, nor relative fluidity, as of a green petal to a crimson petal, a child turned wrong inside her.

4

A stage fills with sixteen men, capable of having everything else thought away and still being
around, like the convenience of a physical theory that works. They imply promise in the contained
silver backing a mirror, not frogs and stars reflected in it, but a descent through clouds at night.
First, moonlight on thick fog, then a glow like blood in the dragonfly wing, then a triangle onto
stars that dwell in the mind in the exact register in which they dwell in themselves, an opening
in the belly of the tall dancer where you look for his eyes, like a green flower on top of a word.
The feeling of insecurity remembered does not appear in steam above the sideboard, nor in the activity
of the potential form of the pond, if he touches her. A young girl holding the hand of a stranger
before your grave, a space of extended courtesy to him, makes a possible error in courtesy.
The music stops. The dancer spills across his form and moves to the edge of the floor in silence.

5

During winter, this had been a matter of stripping meat from the bone, to dry and freeze,
the color of black iris along the edge of a satellite dish. If I dream of shadows of meat
on a white dish like the underside of a leaf, it is a feeling, like thinking. If I imagine
a ghost and a deer, both are true. No one can describe the relation between an experience
that needs to be communicated and the form of communication. It lies next to its form,
separating her, like proximity to death, the way a wild animal automatically lies next to its form.
The metaphor that the eye knows a particular by internalizing its color and shape became
the woman's substitute for animal belief in life among the shades. A metaphor interpreted
as occurrence is her method for only remembering objects which exist in the same size
as their image in her mind, ladyslipper behind the eyesocket, pollen falling through interstices

of her brain cells, as if exact scale were an infallible touchstone for her intention.

Lily pads sketch out of the foreground of the pond. A gossamer, livening fabric tips up alluringly to points of your body, the way a blue wall had assessed the posture of the women. It's why you assume the logical space, "giving a reason," stands in the same relation to the causal emotion for the space, as a halo rescued out of her life.

Daughter

1 (THE DREAM)

An angel swims silently to a flat rock in the night, where seabirds are sleeping, senses them,
and stops. Their recognizing her in the moonlight, without waking, is the physical sensation of meaning
of your dream, when you wake. The birds' dream represents an angel, and later it shelters the meaning,
angel. Royal palms glisten, fronds reaching stars their shape imitates, to show feeling for stars.
The general is concrete, here, in the birds' memories and extends the instinctual limits of their perception,
but this hasn't been recognized, yet.

Holding her face in my hands is holding a bowl from where I was born. The face is not an image
of my feeling, like hills holding sky. The bowl represents his feeling for the immanent structure
of what appears delicate and vulnerable, but is almost inorganic, like feathers. In its own light,
the face seems doughy and opaque, magnolia petals, or my emotion with the rich suggestion of a ruin.

A revolving lighthouse sounds on the island, making pieces of time out of human beings,
with fragrant interstices between lights I consider her time, pleating petal with shadow, until
a petal appears beside a grass blade on the ground, with a beauty unadulterated by any person
who would be beautiful, so I can look around and walk up to a flower without comparing it.

The angel's ribbon fell across her eyes while she was looking at something, a little like light over a wide part in the river, and a little like the pink wall of a house through buds of the trees. It was like these two things, the way yellow on fruit is like a feeling, though this color changes. Your feeling overfills the bowl. I replace it with a gray fledgling in the bowl.

2 (COMMENTARY)

The dream represents a meaning to me. Then, it's a structure that shelters the meaning. My emotion can represent evaluation or contain one, of interaction between an ethereal object and an organism. The angel bows down. There's something like a skeleton among snowflakes about her whiteness, white roots against a muddy bank. It seems her ribcage has turned around to the back. Between front and back, her spirit cannot be expressed, though that's what the front and back mean. You have to accept you don't know the transcendental signified.

To formally express ethereal existence, a relation like reference picks out an entity in the world, such as her. Tulips bloom, lighthouse of pleats. The feeling there's something ineffable it's like to have the person, you can't learn from a sentence about her, is deep or empty. It feels like expectation, space of rocks beyond the island, marked by graceful lamps on points of land like a stage set, *avoiding the rocks,* your relation to time in the future or to other people, like a budded tree. The hunger was satisfied by a physical feeling of meaning on waking from the dream. Tension was relieved without the wish being fulfilled.

Glistening palms among stars are in love with the stars, or are they an intuition identical with stars, a tactile, surface intuition? The place of which I said, "Stars, palms, hunger lie a little distance apart," is a tactile place, if the angel is a vessel of light like skin, or if by tactile proximity of the general in matter, she destroys the frame of my perception, what I meant by "avoiding" the illuminated space. You remember a line of birches next to pine trees, a perfect woman, not her. One sees a latent image reveal itself, something ineffable it's like to be her, getting from a perception to non-perception.

3

Her wings crumple behind her, broken pottery, nautilus shell. The perimeter of the wing bleeds into your consciousness, the idea of an ethereal object, a kind of subterfuge. How mystifying the substantive time is, which had been the transcendental signified! Cherry blossoms precede coppery, energetic leaves. A petal falls on a branch. Leaf opens beside it. What I thought I could lose of a person and what I thought I had lie next to each other, repeating, so the time in which you know her is a foliage during time and folds over on itself, hill filling with dogwood, tree of sky turning rose. A rose angel with the physical sensation of the meaning of your dream, holding a lamp, the waterfall behind her of some contemporary material like cellophane, achieves a cohesive tension exactly beside the contemporary.

Health

1

I cut the stem of the amaryllis, and the water poured out so suddenly, I didn't know what to look at.
There's a blur of force at the cut and a white glare on the table, before the silhouette coalesces.
Light pours out, collapsing the state of the vector of light-potential in the flower or arriving.
The mirror projection of my camera onto an amaryllis gives it geometry I call social space,
in which the ground for physical and etheric bodies photographs. Magic is confusing, if
outside contains inside, so it is not noticed, containment that's symbolic, like numbers.
Their combinatory power makes order, like your unconscious at the level of food, which is pre-symbolic.
As substratum or residue of speech, if she were speaking, her mouth opens out all sorts of presences.

2

Two colors close to each other resonate like presence, the outline of a baby and placenta
on a bed of red leaves. Shadows of leaves blur, as if the small body were attached on
the underside to the image of a uterus, meaning, emotions are abstract. If she's talking
about a physical boundary, orange light collects on the horizon, like an anatomical drawing,

her idea about feeling for a person, the way health is a feeling. He asks you to describe it,
showing you the baby, "Does it feel like this? Without the leaves?" The form of her body
by which she anticipates her power in a dream is light in a tree. It makes the red of leaves.
It's a situation in which light hurts her blood. Looking at the blood makes my eyes tear,
which should be a grille to look through, a continuum of inattention, not like a blood relation.

3

Her self is constructed of units of meaning not given by nature, but successively constituted
by how they're used. The vertical is a woman hanging, uterus between her legs ruffled as a parasol.
The horizontal is a lattice of her concentration toward positive emotion, meaning abstract, but narrative.
Film the woman aging. If you run the film forward or back, you can tell one direction from the other.
If you cut the film into frames, you have a stack of events with one-wayness to them, though nothing
intrinsic to the stack is equivalent to flowing time. This asymmetry is like another person.

4

Define nature as the greatest point of alienation from spirit. Then, nature is her dissolution,
below the threshold of awareness of spirit, an instant cause, not separated by time from a person.
Her speaking reorders events, giving them a sense of necessity to come. Interpretation depends
on subject showing itself as intention or blood relation enmeshed in her, as if the ribcage
were social space. Light on the ground, as through air onto her blue coat is miscible, not private.

You give him the light mesh of your longing, which makes distance blue. It's the same to you, if he's red or blue. You create the idea of a baby and photograph it on red leaves, a blur. You photograph the placenta which dissipates, blue glass feet, your uterus in a jar. Each contains an abstraction of dissolution or flow. As photographs they're spirit. As feet and womb, nature. Even when spirit is not there, you have affection for the form, an outline like heat from a name.

The Four Year Old Girl

I

The "genotype" is her genetic constitution.

The "phenotype" is the observable expression of the genotype as structural and biochemical traits.

Genetic disease is extreme genetic change, against a background of normal variability.

Within the conventional unit we call subjectivity due to individual particulars, what is happening?

She believes she is herself, which isn't complete madness, it's belief.

The problem is not to turn the subject, the effect of the genes, into an entity.

Between her and the displaced gene is another relation, the effect of meaning.

The meaning she's conscious of is contingent, a surface of water in an uninhabited world, existing as our eyes and ears.

You wouldn't think of her form by thinking about water.

You can go in, if you don't encounter anything.

Though we call heavy sense impressions stress, all impression creates limitation.

I believe opaque inheritance accounts for the limits of her memory.

The mental impulse is a thought and a molecule tied together, like sides of a coin.

A girl says sweetly, it's time you begin to look after me, so I may seem lovable to myself.

She's inspired to change the genotype, because the cell's memory outlives the cell.

It's a memory that builds some matter around itself, like time.

2

Feelings of helplessness drove me to fantastic and ridiculous extremes.
Nevertheless, the axis of her helplessness is not the axis I grasp when I consider it a function of inheritance.
Chromatin fails to condense during mitosis.
A fragile site recombines misaligned genes of the repeated sequence.
She seems a little unformed, gauze stretches across her face, eyelids droop.
When excited, she cries like a cat and fully exhibits the "happy puppet" syndrome.
Note short fingers and hypoplastic painted nails.
Insofar as fate is of real order here, signifying embodiment, the perceived was present in the womb.
A gap or cause presents to any apprehension of attachment.
In her case, there's purity untainted by force or cause, like the life force.
Where, generically, function creates the mother, in this case it won't even explain this area.
She screams at her.
A species survives in the form of a girl asking sweetly.
Nevertheless, survival of the species as a whole has meaning.
Each girl is transitory.

3

Her focus extends from in front of her into distance, so she's not involved in what she looks at.
Rhodopsin in the unaffected gene converts photons to retinal impulse, so she sees normally for years.
The image, the effects of energy starting from a real point, is reflected on a surface, lake or area of the
    occipital lobe.

You don't need the whole surface to be aware of a figure, just for some points of real space to correspond to effect at other points.

There's an image and a struggle to recognize reception of it.

She sees waves and the horizon as if she were water in the water.

The mother's not looking at her daughter from the place from which the daughter sees her.

She doesn't recognize abnormal attributes.

The daughter resolves her mother as fire in the woods, red silk.

In the waiting room, she hopes a large dog will walk up to her, be kind and fulfill her wishes.

Between what occurs by chance and, "Mother, can you see I'm dying?" is the same relation we deal with in recurrence.

Is not what emerges from the anxiety of her speech, their most intimate relation, beyond death, which is their chance?

Obedience to one's child is anxious, heartfelt, but not continuous, like a white mote in her eye.

Within the range of deteriorating sight, in which sight will be her memory, disobedience moves toward unconsciousness.

4

Her skull is large and soft to touch.

The thoracic cavity small, limbs short, deformed and vertebrae flattened.

All the bones are under-mineralized.

Bluish light surrounds her.

This theme concerns her status, since she doesn't place her inheritance in a position of subjectivity, but of an object.

Her X-ray teems with energy, but locked outside material.

One creates a mouse model of human disease by disrupting a normal mouse gene in vitro, then injecting
the mutated gene into host embryos.
DNA integrated into the mouse genome is expressed and transmitted to progeny.
Like touch, one cell can initiate therapy.
The phenotype, whose main task is to transform everything into secondary, kinetic energy, pleasure,
innocence, won't define every subject.
The mother's genotype makes a parallel reality to her reality, now.
She stands over her and screams.
That the exchange is unreal, not imaginary, doesn't prevent the organ from embodying itself.
By transferring functional copies of the gene to her, he can correct the mutant phenotype, lightly touching
the bad mother, before.

5

On her fourth birthday, a rash on the elbow indicated enzyme deficiency.
Her view folded inward.
Ideas about life from experience are no use in the unfolding of a potential, empty and light, though there's
still potential for phenomena to be experienced.
A moment of seeing can intervene like a suture between an image and its word.
An act is no longer structured by a real that's not caught up in it.
Instead of denying material, I could symbolize it with this mucus and its trailings.
The moment the imaginary exists, it creates its own setting, but not the same way as form at the intuitive
level of her mother's comprehension.
In all comprehension, there's an error, forgetting the creativity of material in its nascent form.
So, you see in her eyes her form of compassion for beings who perceive suffering as a real substrate.

6

Mother must have done something terrible, to be so bereaved.

Ambiguity of a form derives from its representing the girl, full of capability, saturated with love.

If the opposite of possible is real, she defines real as impossible, her real inability to repeat the child's game, over and over.

Parallel woven lines of the blanket extend to water.

Just a hint of childish ferocity gives them weight.

At night, inspiration fell on her like rain, penetrating the subject at the germline, like a navel.

Joy at birth, a compaction of potential and no potential, is an abstraction that was fully realized.

Reducing a parent to the universality of signifier produces serene detachment in her, abstract as an electron micrograph of protein-deplete human metaphase DNA.

Its materiality is a teletransport of signified protoplasm across lineage or time, avid, muscular and compact, as if pervasive, attached to her, *in* a particular matriarchy of natural disaster, in which the luminosity of a fetal sonogram becomes clairvoyant.

The love has no quantity or value, but only lasts a length of time, different time, across which unfolds her singularity without compromising life as a whole.

The Doll

Discourse on death contains a rhetoric of borders.

Shape delimits your right of absolute property, existence, tracing your traits as the border of what belongs to you.

You don't have to touch the border to know how it feels, whether a napkin or a rose petal feels softer, the border between you, or the end of her life.

Compare these in your mind, without locating the border or experiencing death, using a subtler sense of contact, subtlety that's part of a thing.

The image of a rose grows fainter until only screen is left.

As soon as the whole is determined by wanting her to stay, she's no longer what she feels she is, not determinable.

Something abstract becomes a part.

2

A mountain touches a cloud in clear sky, acquiring otherworldliness from light on the cloud.
It has volume like a crystal, but weighs like a cardinal point.
The lighted flank is revealed as distinct shape, so shape becomes a fragment.
You drive toward it, as the approach of the person.
As soon as she's named, her presence can cross a threshold, whether she arrives physically.
You photograph her doll, cut out the doll's head, enlarge to original size, and get the whole doll, the way
    her mind realizes possibility, as if the doll thought, and the girl became space and direction for it.

3

The woman in the shape of a rock and its shadow by a tree is a whole that can stretch, when light is
    lateral like consciousness.
Light from above the tree casts a pinwheel around the trunk.
Even in shadow, light contains the past of waves which came from everywhere to reach that part.
She touches her collar.
The sleeper grows fainter on the screen.
Either images are real, and time between is abstract, or this image of her marks real time.
Her interval, like the stars, is real.
They've no alterity with respect to themselves.

4

She lies down with the animals, flowering trees, magicians.
Common measure between her and the screen is an irrational number.
I employ two symbolized realities, so connecting paths traversed by light make an edge.
We're the other for this boundary.
It occurs through physical contact, like a part detailed as the whole, as if a series of frames were the same as movement.
When you change this point of space to a point in time, middle ground appears.
Her dream is wonderful as a falling star of the whole.
I want to locate the ineffable beyond middle ground.

5

The doll consists of a tangerine, stem and two leaves for its head, a body of a potato, striped sticks for arms, and some lace around the potato.
Flesh that's not suffering has form, occupying a subtle space that contains its own intuition.
Inasmuch as it's formless, it doesn't provoke anxiety.
If this little image is all there is, and space around of no significance, we've the usual view of fragmentation.
The line between thing and event transcends order, not the perimeter of a lesion in a photograph, a case in which she'd so many fragments to hold together, what holds became disorganized, not abstract.

6

Cool crystal until electrons go through, as if it were dead.
Light goes through branches of the tree, oxygenating blood.
She sleeps in a red gown.
People around her are the size of rabbits and birds.
Tree trunks, water, people's clothing moved like waves.
The dragon moves from a tendency to real occurrence.
Nothing's needed to go there, because my memory's not found at any site.
She fades to the origin of the senses, variations of a person who both inhabits a ghost and co-habits with it,
    temporarily.
Nightlights flash at this border.

7

It trembles in unstable multiplicity of no context to stop it, like a footprint.
An animal, running, leaps over me.
Rocks in the sun laterally represent constellations and their shadows.
You could say the extent of her being can map onto knowing, so being and knowing are identical in the
    infinity.
The lighted boundary, at which an interval is apprehended beyond its image or word, is experience
    characterized by our relation.
I mean, you are beyond subjectivity.
There's an opposition, a work of mourning.
There's a mirror relation, one beyond the other, an animal, like a resplendent bird, unfolded for her in the
    animal's space.

8

What if the only concept of an interval were *now,* moon behind clouds the same as a lesion?
What if opposing another concept to presence were impractical as a border?
The interval collapses from tendency to occurrence.
The misty, lighted edge calls for endurance or bliss other than opposing from both sides of a line, a part
    with no context for which is softer, light or the animal?
It makes me hesitate, as between poles of an alternative, like a peacock, the way non-duality looks in the
    face of her longing, to a mother inconsolable before a blessing.

Kali

1

First, the beginning, pre-supposed as a past, goes to ground like a foundation and doubles itself.
Then, I defy inflection, in having this double outside itself.
It becomes a name, the black of an eye, a person you fear, but it's not yet in the world or fixed in time.
Black means she's unknown by people full of ignorance, since it stands for their ignorance.
Figures on a white bowl in a basin of milk come alive, white dog attacking a bear for spectators.
Its dark color is the density, when she substitutes her own gesture, given sense by my compliance.
Sense becomes a potential real space, following her like a drift of things.
Vertiginous animality tangles in pleated material of my body.
An animal mother creates a matter double for her.
Its matter is ground, blue to blackness, bare as dread reality.

2

The ghost limb is determined from outside, since it derives from a violent incident, but unified inside by
    originary structures in the brain stem and limbic system.
She stands in front of waves like a stone on a reflecting surface.

The ungroundedness of a wave constitutes the violence of sacrifice.

A triangle places itself on the sea, sometimes obscuring the woman, like a witch's hat.

The hat, existing "in the air" on what you see, omits what was natural in itself.

Fate, an airy image, shakes her from sleep and transforms what you see into a beach of witches.

Is realization in matter also required, because folds in matter might re-duplicate the folds in her clothes?

3

Now at night preserves itself as a black bird.

Form is its principle, a trace in dark of a body that couldn't be sensed.

Her being there opens out of her captivity in me, to being like swimming.

Experience of her shifts like a pronoun or originary transcendence and is specified through some other thing, surface of emergence (motherhood, environment).

"I" means a pronoun for who's speaking, so "I" cannot mean the witch.

The witch relates to "I" as an index, briefly creating the illusion, need doesn't exist.

Prayer, undisturbed by clamor, is not dragged in the mud, but entrusted to memory.

It goes to the ground and disappears.

When she threw snow at the bird on the road, it never moved.

The pronoun, whiteness, moved downward.

4

She spans a bridge over a human being.

She appears black from a distance, the way sky appears blue, but held in your hand is colorless like larvae or an element of the voice.

Use crystals to identify this seed element introduced into my body, as if by genetic index.

Matter becomes a matter of my expression.

A fold in matter relates to the light of memory, the way the fold catches illumination and varies, according to the light of day.

How does a fold determine "thin" and superimposable depth, the paper fold defining a "minimum" of depth on our scale, as the image of a pleated fan casts a sense of depth in front of the image of a wall?

The cerebral cortex, gray matter, is a large sheet of two-dimensional tissue, wadded up to fit in the spherical skull.

A room transforms itself into two dimensions, into consciousness, following a line, like the proliferation of the symbol for her dark skin.

We're made to believe she is the thing *per se,* she is the picture.

5

Red flowers amid dark light reflecting from a plane of water drying up, lamella, *maya,* as if there were nothing prior for the girl, only this chaotic visual from which a symbol takes its volume.

When the perception achieves speed, a wave becomes hard as a wall of marble.

You learn from seeing the pain and humiliation on her face and thinking you caused it.

If everything black embodies her as time, like a wall of black marble, how to think of black itself?

Is it the point of enactment from a symbol?

6

I don't care for this artificial layer anymore.

Now my mother is dead and dark as the animal's eyes.

Her symbol, which has neither sound nor thought of sound, is the word for the thing which I inwardly
speak by seeing it, but can't see it and can't say it.

Her gown glows like crystal.

The light wall lends her refinement and immateriality.

Nevertheless, her expressiveness maintains through a place that's neither sensible nor the unity of a
synthesis, like stains on patterned cloth around her.

The selvedge is sprocketed, strip of film, polka dots, her pupils, setting point of view.

A length of cloth would localize in space elements distributed across time.

Love was not a sentiment, because in nature, this pattern had no place.

In me, nothingness utilized the pattern as a mnemonic aid, but a pattern can change.

7

The bear bleeds on the white dog.

Its soul is the collected thoughts and feelings of the spectators.

"Auto"-sentimentality conveys this projection of her internal space into the arena.

Separability of parts applies to abstract matter, not pleats of mass that surround living beings, but veins
like a witch in the soul.

She pops out of a planet in a cartoon, moving around earth, above my body.

Pleats hold her like an animal in the dark we hear rustle away without calling it.

It returns from a dark eye, intuited like space at rest, dissolved of every other of time, bad infinity, thought of time.

So bad was your luck, though looking, you did not see the woman came as your daughter with bound feet.

The witch, my control like medicine, did not end as a narrative fold in matter, since this communication stretches indefinitely, absolute achieving potential.

When the spectacle reached its climax, a shape glowed blue violet in the halo of the ionization.

Fingernails coated with oil were used for this prophecy.

Permanent Home

1

I seek a permanent home, but this structure has an appearance of indifferent compoundedness and isolation, heading toward hopelessness.

The boy pulls an animal on a leash.

The house with a red roof rests between two hills.

I can look through its windows to the sea.

His aggression opposes what in a domestic animal, cold open space, large enough to work with isolation?

House is the projection, space around it intermediary, theater.

You don't have to consume the space to exist, distance, point-to-point, in which a beloved ruin is middle ground, for example.

2

First house and space negate one another.

Then, they're a series.

The boy watches a mouse run around the rim of a lampshade.

He relates wanting to catch a mouse with the room, ground.

Wanting a master image obscures ground, like objects in space.

House and space are composite, like my dream, a bubble, lightning, starting point and any second place.

3

Rain pours out a gutter onto the poor horse.

Horse runs under a tin roof supported by poles.

Stockpiles of beams, salvaged wood, brick melt into contextless waste.

I understand the situation by perceiving parts, one after another, then reversing in a glance that removes time.

So, I can intuit contextless waste as ground.

4

The water tank sits on a frame of used wood, like a packing crate.

I look through it to an extinct volcano.

The panorama is true figuratively as space, and literally in a glass wall, where clouds appear like flowers, and the back-lit silhouette of a horse passes by.

A file of evergreens secures the cliff amid debris from a crew building, as at the edge of the sea.

Oranges, dumplings, boiled eggs take on the opaque energy of a stranger.

Knowledge as lintel, bond beam (model signs) holds the world at a distance.

A master image like bone condenses from the indistinct point-to-point feeling of self with which construction began.

My house returns from outside, as if my spirit had been blocking my path, when I wasn't going anywhere in particular.

5

Materials and freedom combine, so materials aren't subjective.

The material of space is like having a skeleton to gain a vantage point on seamless distance, as in a comparison.

It's a style of accumulating materials that does not become a solid thing, anymore.

Accommodating a view by being able to be seen through is perceptual, not abstract, like space painted white.

Give a house the form of an event.

Relate it to something there, a form of compassion.

Your point of view is: it's solid already, so there's warmth.

In this primitive situation, pure form translates a former empire of space as wilderness.

Chinese space breaks free from the view in front of me, while my house continues to rotate on earth.

Dressing Up Our Pets

I

I sew a bright hood for my pet mouse.

I make holes for the eyes, the nose and ears.

I stand it on two legs and it stands on its own, a while.

My friend, the white mouse, is iridescent, not an image that began in my intuition as ready-found material.

I sew a hood for the rabbit, eye and nose holes, sheathed ears.

Its movement, the difference between a thing and its color, burdens of our activity of dressing pets.

The mouse is old, but its image is light.

Between its alleged color and its alleged visibility is a lining, like the double of a mouse, latency, flesh.

The surface of the visibility of a family doubles over its whole extension with invisible reserve.

In my flesh what's visible, by refolding or padding, exhibits *their* being as the complement of possibility.

Since possibility is this situation as thought, as a universal.

2

The sun distributes onto desert below us.

Small trees are distributed, but not integrated.

Moonlight distributes *and* integrates.

Pines on a crest at dusk, separate figures, will become imageless, integration of all the black trees, black animals, etc., night animals, domestic animals waiting at home.

These innocents from nature are my attempt to draw near sacred feeling without others present, who, as unending movement, consume tranquil ground.

Then, ground becomes like other people.

It's why I remember a span of light, not because of satisfaction, but framing, an interruption that will inhabit me, like what happened the other day, when he forgot me.

We were shopping, and he just went on.

Ordinarily, I wouldn't be sensitive, but that day, the usual stimulation, looking at fruits and vegetables, seemed to belong to him.

I also should have experience, for how would I make my selection?

3

"How old are you . . . have seen a lot . . . you wait still . . . hard to see . . ."

The audience integrates a man singing with what's visible behind them.

He delicately rotates his hands to an emotion that's like a place.

His age and our suffering became a concrete node of things happening at once and things, one after another.

He is not real like a star, but he has his own impetus of how the song goes at dusk.

So, you think his song caused your sad feeling, like your hand touching your hand.

A girl sings along without knowing the words, entering memory.

That there's no present of what will happen to her, is your expectation.

Everyone becomes great in proportion to a singer's spurious expectations, like good mistakes.

4

Parachute on the desert, blue-white with light, eleven sheep head-to-head in a circle, asleep.

Enjoyment and substance in real time involve clearings about which pivot opaque zones.

Real is a span of visibility, inasmuch as your flesh is not chaotic, *of* a contingency.

The real thing substitutes for another who's not representable, as he gathers up parachute and delivery.

If I stay here and you mean something, the part in common is disjunct from what you mean, like my hands touching.

That you're telepathic means nothing; you've facts you can't know, which still work in connections of my experience.

A rock in rain distributing water along texture is my response to experience.

Inasmuch as your flesh is an interplay of disjunctions needed for identity, flesh is texture.

Our meeting occurs near a hill you climb every day to water transplanted irises.

Why don't you let others do that?

5

Although I do not wish to separate from him, now, due to faults of compound phenomena being demonstrated, he will disappear from my sight and hearing.

The beauty of his song derives from the fact: it represents something to someone.

Any family that's concentrated, insofar as it represents something, may be taken for someone.

Wherever there's waiting is this transference.

The danger is: you'll be deceived by the metonymy of my tender feeling, light and multiple.

You go to pick up the child after school.

You remain a few moments, talking with a teacher beside the loom.

Why are you telling her this?

* * * * * * * *

Glory, formless substance, circular dawn, a child's drawing of stars, or snowflakes and lines.

Each line connects, so it's the same star falling, loop the loop.

And each line belongs to each star, my friend the white rabbit, little mouse, squirrel, impatient, shaking off their clothes.

I Love Morning

We're in New Mexico.

It's summer—all morning to lounge in bed, talk on the phone, read the paper.

Martha pats her spiky old cat, Manet, studies cat's cradle from a book.

Time is ethos, as if we're engendered by our manner in it, not required to be in ourselves.

With no cause to act on time, there's no pointing beyond, so he gets up and plays Scarlatti in his underwear.

Being together, like scrim, defocuses space.

Knowability (features) of her face, continually passing into expression, is a para-existence beside the mother, halo, unraveling.

Light increases toward the red spectrum of day.

She nurses her cat with a syringe supported against my large arm.

My body is a film on her preconscious of images she chooses to line conversation.

Its alterity becomes a nuance of our ineluctable situation of futons, dishes, books, with the potential of a destabilized surface of time, no outflow through pink walls.

Atmospheric presence soaks objects.

2

I'm making a puzzle of the New York subway map for her.

I replace each stop with a name from our family, pestering for more names, Schmidt, Laubach.

I should see family as bodhisattvas helping me on the path, but it's difficult if I'm not a bodhisattva myself, to recognize one.

Anyone entering by chance (UPS, neighbor child) sees synchrony, confusion emanate from our bodies of smiling individuals, as if photographed separately, then assembled.

Asymmetry of legs, human, animal, disjunctions among gestures are sheathed in rose light wafting around us a physical promise of happiness.

She sets up a tent in our room, paints on the inside names of all the people she's known, like stars.

She cuts out paper flowers and scatters them on the floor of the tent, morning not interfering, even though flowers are immediate, universal.

I love to read newspapers.

Negative space enters my house like spirits, low pressure under a table, in the petals of a rose, like a person you love.

Maternal love is needed for the spatial sense, which gives rise to infant laughter.

A ringing, overflowing sense of others collapses us, with no representable condition of belonging.

She interviews him on tape and he answers in the voice of a young girl.

She draws Manet as average, general, to protect him, then introduces many toy animals into the tent.

3

A common mistake of groups is requiring each one to compensate for lacks in the whole, to care at any cost.

Our coalescence around a sick pet overflows (like laughter), incommensurate with problems of sociality in her terrifying dream.

The dream is intermediary, unraveling a thing beside itself.

I should try to help her, whether or not I truly help.

Kisses from the Moon

I

I'm so pleased to be friends with Maryanne, though I don't understand how she has time for me, with her many friends.

The event of friendship opens, making afterward a field of possibility from which to begin, tenderness pre-existing.

At my party, how does friendship sometimes light her being there, sometimes possibility itself?

Let the sensation, "I listen to her," dissolve in my head; there's no self.

What's called *hearer* is *hearing*.

An exemplary listener is determined, who pre-exists my wish to be heard.

She loses this presumed identity through singular beauty, one dividing the other.

Perhaps, "Can you hear me in the night?" exaggerates friendship.

Its featherweight vulnerability offers no counterweight for her care through that night?

I speak to you; I promise, I say something; listen to me.

Hearing attunes to an open place, window, absence, a stranger's arrhythmic walk in open time, then my walk.

There's no kiss from the moon except through this window, no rhythmic interstices between steps, as outside draws near, only surface on space, possibility.

My friend exists in my sight.

Lightning, then blindness when she can't be distinguished from open space.

Moon unifies my empty room with this space.

Afterwards, illness kept me aloof.

Now, I know better; community's not meant to protect me; it's exposure to others, a window.

I make them into feathers of my desire for you, first forgetting to leave, then arriving at your party.

I lay my head on my arms on a glass table, suppressed admiration attaching to me, like surface touching moonlight.

I have to re-create the scene at a distance, so I can watch.

At the podium, I say in my head, "I love you, be my friends, exchange these promises, you to whom I aspire."

Nest

1

My mother tongue, Chinese, has an immemorial history before me.

I was inserted into it, a motive for my language.

I learned it naturally, filling it with intentions, and will leave it without intent for other children.

My mother and I speak local language and sometimes our mother tongue, as in my dream, with its intent.

What to intend in changing the mother tongue of my daughter, compassion, not being ill, sleep in which a daughter resonates depth, like a bell.

"Loving the wind" is equivalent to intention as rhetorical surface, like writing my diary on her skin.

Non-comprehension tips ambivalent matter, as if there were two of us, here: one is Kuan Yin, one is mother tongue.

Her matter inserted, a motive, is always somewhere else, exiting one language, another without intent, translated as heart.

2

I want to tell you what's difficult to admit, that I left home.

Change of mother tongue between us activates an immunity, margin where dwelling and travel are not distinct.

Artifacts throw themselves toward light without becoming signification.

Telling you is not an edge of the light.

There's no margin of a shadow to imply interior.

In my childhood house was a deep porch covered with vines.

Look past our silhouette to silhouettes (like shadows) of guests arriving in a bright yard.

Light in the next room falls on her, as she bends to kiss you.

Skylight pours down, then covers the mud wall, like cloth.

I observe a lighted field seem to hang in space in front of me.

Speaking, not filling in, surface intent, is a cabinet of artifacts, comparisons, incongruity.

3

My origin is a linguistic surface like a decorated wall, no little houses at dusk, yellow lights coming on, physical, mute.

Its significance is received outside hearing, decorating simply by opening the view.

Wherever I look is prior absence, no figure, ruin escaping an aesthetic: hammock, electric fan, ghost don't qualify as guards.

The comfortable interior my guest inhabits is a moving base, states of dwelling undetermined, walls cross-hatched like mother tongue.

The foreign woman occupies a home that's impersonal, like the nest of a parasite.

Its value is contentless but photographable, in the context of an indigenous population, tipping between physical ease and the freedom of animals accumulating risk.

When the scene is complex, I turn to the audience and comment aloud, then return to room and language at hand, weakened by whoever didn't hear me, as if I don't recognize the room, because my family moved in, while I was away.

Text imbricated with outside, a wall is waves.

So, I decorate in new mother tongue, plasticity of fragment, cool music.

There's a lock in it, *of* the surface.

It still lights apricots in bloom, leaves, skins of organisms, horizon, borders that represent places.

4

A margin can't rot, no bloated outline around memories of witnesses, the way origin in the present is riddled with holes.

Pick one and slip through it, like a girl whose body is changing.

Domestic space oozes light through a loophole, mother to mother, so close I can't catch it through myself.

My family is vulnerable at the margin, child, line of a cheek diffusing energy, line of her eye extending an inner look.

Don't let her ooze through loopholes we inhabit like migrants, light drifting across five windows on the river, drifting functioning as imagination so intimate our space seems anonymous.

Furnishings, colors are sumptuous in relation to anonymity, textiles like money.

5

I feel the right to have my invitation accepted, an open house.

Guests appear in other places for other occasions with my invitation, pleading for the secular, the empathic.

Speaking, an artifact, creates a loophole for no rapport, no kinship, no education, on a frontier where wild is a margin of style, and rhetoric's outside that.

In this case, she'd immigrated long ago, so they tried to stay with her as a family.

Speech opens onto a lost plain, then contracts to a diffuse margin between metaphor for space and concept of drunk, ill, running away.

Her story begins aesthetically, but hysterical acts withdraw it to a floating space of frustration, unself, and a paranoid husband is produced.

Her words are high-handed, awkward, formal.

He hears them as expressions of personal pique and self-indulgence, but won't say she uses power unfairly in the pose of unhappy mother.

Such topics are prohibited except at the kitchen table, in the car, etc.

It's said, illustrious persons lead parallel lives, which join in eternity, but some lives veer off the straight path to community.

So, I speak with care, but prove authority won't take me far, because the area's too large.

In this, daughter, you see more than I did at your age, because you see me.

Hearing

1

A voice with no one speaking, like the sea, merges with my listening, as if imagining her thinking about me makes me real.

Its matter is attributed to its passing away, a transcendence whose origin has come apart.

She can't hear me hearing her, sits informally, elbow on knee, circling real with matter, possible form, for which being touched is a condition of composition.

Her basis starts uncontrived; stone on a path exerts pressure on a surface, hand rests on a child's head.

She's not speaking words I hear in an undertone.

The loved one's face radiates a secret the lover touches and distributes to all the places of a stone, bruised foot, barrier for an insect, dirt occupied by its shadow, like a cut ornament.

My hearing touches my limit on all sides, a community exposed.

Hearing: transparency arms arc over, glass nest for her young.

2

A bird falls out of the air, through the anti-weave, into the anti-net, delineating anti-immanence.

Twenty-four crows upstate, each fall is a gestural syllable.

Cover them with a blue cloth of creatures ready to be born, contact like starlight that will arrive, for sure.

Let mothers catch them, raccoon, Labrador bitch, girl, inter-species conservative mothers, arms out like foliage, no locomotion of their own.

Her matter is spacing in the present, as I come along or go away.

It's experienced as vague, general understanding, not accessible.

That's how a girl away is undivided, like virtuous deeds accomplished quietly.

Her flashing sequins are an unapplied form of universal, co-presence before space, internal line of time into hearing not arriving from meanings of words, like starlight.

She spans real time over this sense of being touched, like a beautiful dress.

3

It's response, not perspective.

The plane tips up and completes our world with transparency, synapse between a birdcall and hearing it, pink and shade facets of waves, butterfly on tongue.

The light is not real like a collected object, but its direct, concrete application warms real things.

The potlach settles around me in a house, designating an exterior toward you, not endowing stone with interior.

That depends on deep matter, for which a woman opts for deep acting, suppressing irritation at demands of family by inventing reasons to sympathize with those boors, to feel sincere though alienated from her bodily expression, screen simulation.

Light goes through it to the plane of the sea, of mother tongue.

In nothing in the beautiful room could I recognize myself.

A non-transparent self is needed, an aesthetics of documentation in which images have power, because the drama is real.

They withdraw from matter to representation, for more agency, point of presence, bird falling along a stitched in-and-out of my hearing it call and its ceasing to exist.

4

I found I could take words from one discipline and intersect them with another, such as generous feeling with listening to supplicants.

Empty space intersects with the dignity of stars, of homelessness, health ruined by addiction, to help supplicants—

Trying to be part of the neighborhood, school activism, etc., with a serene demeanor not caught in form of fairy or butterfly wing calmly breathing, alternating with the physical situation, someone ill, someone tortured.

Hearing is the fractality of fragments occurring (as they disintegrate).

Immanence is outside that as absence of the totality of fragments.

Her body (translucence, colored leaves) is a surface you try to make transparent, uninscribed, unlined by good deeds, abstaining from lineage.

Join lineation and surface of her body by voice and hearing, small animals, fragments swept away, lost colors of refractions inside cells, feathers, albino, crepe de Chine.

Hearing as good annuls being toward another.

It gathers good aesthetically into relationship like a figure, her body you remember, as in a family, space behind each person.

During her last weeks, Madame reached the end of memory.

Present and future shed perspective, so birds flying away remained the same size, although her gaze, in memory, on beloved children retained the physical latency of hearing them.

Audience

1

People think, at the theater, an audience is tricked into believing it's looking at life.

The film image is so large, it goes straight into your head.

There's no room to be aware of or interested in people around you.

Girls and cool devices draw audience, but unraveling the life of a real human brings the outsiders.

I wrote before production began, "I want to include all of myself, a heartbroken person who hasn't worked for years, who's simply not dead."

Many fans feel robbed and ask, "What kind of show's about one person's unresolved soul?"

2

There's sympathy for suffering, also artificiality.

Having limbs blown off is some person's reality, but not mine.

I didn't want to use sympathy for others as a way through my problems.

There's a gap between an audience and particulars, but one can be satisfied by particulars, on several levels: social commentary, sleazy fantasy.

Where my film runs into another's real life conditions seems problematic, but they don't link with me.

The linking is the flow of images, thwarting a fan's transference.

If you have empathy to place yourself in my real situation of face-to-face intensity, then there would be no mirror, not as here.

3

My story is about the human race in conflict with itself and nature.

An empathic princess negotiates peace between nations and huge creatures in the wild.

I grapple with the theme, again and again.

Impatience and frustration build among fans.

"She achieves a personal voice almost autistic in lack of affect, making ambiguous her well-known power to communicate emotion, yet accusing a system that mistakes what she says."

Sex, tech are portrayed with lightness, a lack of divisions that cause anxieties elsewhere.

When I find a gap, I don't fix it, don't intrude like a violent, stray dog, separating flow and context, to conform what I say to what you see.

Time before the show was fabulous, blank.

When I return, as to an object in space, my experience is sweeter, not because of memory.

The screen is a mirror where a butterfly tries so hard not to lose the sequence of the last moments.

I thought my work should reflect society, like mirrors in a cafe, double-space.

There's limited time, but we *feel* through film media we've more.

4

When society deterritorialized our world with money, we managed our depression via many deterritorializations.

Feeling became vague, with impersonal, spectacular equivalents in film.

My animator draws beautifully, but can't read or write.

He has fears, which might become reality; Godzilla *is* reality.

When I saw the real princess, I thought her face inauspicious, ill-favored, but since I'd heard she was lovely, I said, "Maybe she's not photogenic today."

Compared to my boredom, I wondered if her life were not like looking into a stream at a stone, while water rushed over me.

I told her to look at me, so her looking is what everything rushes around.

I don't care about story, *look*, so much as, what do you think of her? Do you like her?

She's not representative because of gaps in the emotion, only yummy parts, and dialogue that repeats.

She pencils a black line down the back of her leg.

A gesture turns transparent and proliferates into thousands of us doing the same.

Acknowledging the potential of a fan club, she jokingly describes it as "suspect."

She means the performance comes out through the noise.

5

At the bar, you see a man catch hold of a girl by the hair and kick her.

You could understand both points of view, but in reality, no.

You intervene, feeling shame for hoping someone else will.

It becomes an atmosphere, a situation, by which I mean, groups.

In school we're taught the world is round, and with our own eyes we confirmed a small part of what we could imagine.

Because you're sitting in a dark place, and I'm illuminated, and a lot of eyes are directed at me, I can be seen more clearly than if I mingled with you, as when we were in high school.

We were young girls wanting to describe love and to look at it from outer space.

Safety

Increasingly in our world, forgiveness is asked for, granted, withheld, face-to-face or below the surface, like slow combustion, and I need to elucidate the chain of oxidation.

You fill around the open space of our being here, tensile welds, not empty in the sense, a weld yields.

The pathetic story is removed from calculation.

Yet, banality in identifying with others is no cause for pathos to dissolve.

So, I continue to calculate my house, its significance as a holding place for something to look at (image, word), building would illustrate.

I saw, when a building falls, interior remains interior.

Then, individuals acquire that same size.

Also, the innateness of being a witness annexes size, by seeing putting you next to.

I mean, immense size.

One folds in and re-opens to outside, not "as if" building for someone afraid of heights, who strains long, structural tresses of light, trying to wear out an image.

Safety

The photograph is handsome of the young man.

Points of likeness puncture the surface of my sight, absent person I bring inside from an interior he inhabits as friend, i.e., innate, strange, as in artificial light.

Neighbor by neighbor, a composition not inscribed in framed space, now haunts it.

Piece comes from you (referent) in me, safe house for the virtual as possible, with unlocatable brightness and clarity.

Ground is the beginning, how I remember you by its lack of a basis on which to found, instant replay, afterimage hollowed out in advance, your family who feels secure, their voices.

Don't be afraid to see something you don't want to see.

What if the beginning has no motion, just size, height?

Follow this line.

Your fear of coming to the end is relieved, when you look back through its hollowness.

You see receding X's, joints, (forever) connect the line to its interior (witness), as what fills a space, what arcs it away?

Safety

Urban space is a series of partial views, convex, opaque.

You go from mass to detail, individuals, little ants.

The instinct to preserve oneself deflects onto vertigo from the domination of space, fear of death to fear of damage to the beautiful body.

You connect dwelling to a child guarded by a woman.

Its fate is foretold, child implicit in a word chain, flash, flowers in ice.

In the days we have left, we count our probable meetings, first surface content, then in your language, as in my dream.

The more disconnected your monologue, the more it correlates to something latent in that moment, separation, flowers in ice.

It's not raining, but it's as if there were mud everywhere, and you're plastered in mud.

When a person falls in front of you, something like rain washes mud away, and his leg becomes white as a piece of marble.

Being with each other, we want to reveal and reveal, conceal nothing, but there's the sense something does not get across, a secret.

In this sense, hospitality between us is a secret interior, instead of reality being the plaintiff's.

Shards, detail, singularity, winter garden in glass, palms, extreme refinement of the civility.

There's a linking of structure by joint and weld, springiness, and an unlinking across expanse.

The rigor of the link is an artifact.

Its volume is innate in the witness, leg covered over, memorialized by what I saw, concealed, closed, covered with sight as with gauze, light surface with which I wrap you, light trampoline.

I Love Artists

1

I go to her house and talk with her as she draws me or knits, so it's not one-on-one exactly, blue tattooed stars on her feet.

I pull the knitted garment over my head to my ankles.

Even if a detail resists all significance or function, it's not useless, precisely.

I describe what could happen, what a person probably or possibly does in a situation.

Nothing prevents what happens from according with what's probable, necessary.

A chance occurrence is remarkable, when it appears to happen by design.

2

Telling was engendered in my body and fell upon me, like a battle skimming across combatants, a bird hovering.

Beautiful friends stopped dressing; there was war.

I'd weep, then suddenly feel joy and sing loud words from another language, not knowing my song's end.

I saw through an event and its light shone through me.

Before, indifference was: black nothingness, that indeterminate animal in which everything is dissolved; and white nothingness, calm surface of floating, unconnected determinations.

Imagine something, which distinguishes itself, yet that from which it distinguishes does not distinguish itself from it.

Lightning distinguishes itself from black sky, but trails behind, as if distinguishing itself from what espouses it.

When ground rises to the surface, her form decomposes in this mirror in which determination and the indeterminate combine.

Did you know, finally, there was not communication between her and myself?

Communication was in time and space that were coming anyway.

I may suffer if I can't tell the agony of a poisoned rat, as if I were biting.

3

Bruce leaving for the night makes space for his cat to enter.

Mouse (left) exits door and returns.

Moth and mouse on sculpture exit (left), noise.

It's an exterior relation, like a conducting wire, light fragment by fragment.

I realize my seeing is influenced by him, for example, when we change form and become light reaching into corners of the room.

Even now, we're slipping into shadows of possessions that day by day absorb our energy.

I left my camera on to map unfinished work with shimmering paths of my cat (now disappeared), mice and moths (now dead).

There's space in a cat walking across the room, like pages in a flip-book.

The gaps create a reservoir in which I diffuse my embarrassment at emotion for animals.

I posted frames each week, then packed them into suitcases, the white cat and her shadow, a black cat.

I named her Watteau, who imbues with the transitory friendship we saw as enduring space in a forest.

4

A level of meaning can be the same as a place.

Then you move to your destination or person along that plane.

Arriving doesn't occur from one point to the next.

It's the difference in potential, a throw of dice, which necessarily wins, since charm as of her handcrafted gift affirms chance.

I laugh when things coming together by chance seem planned.

You move to abandon time brackets, water you slip into, what could bring a sliding sound of the perimeter of a stone?

You retain "early" and "walking" as him in space.

When a man becomes an animal, with no resemblance between them, it feels tender.

When a story is disrupted by analyzing too much, elements can be used by a witch's need for disharmony.

My advice to you is, don't get lost too deep in need, unless you're going to join the witches.

Creation is endless.

Your need would be as if you were a white animal pulling yourself into a tree in winter, and your tears draw a line on the snow.

Concordance

I

Writing encounters one who does not write and I don't try for him, but face-to-face draw you onto a line or flight like a break that may be extended, the way milkweed filling space above the field is "like" reading.

Then, it's possible to undo misunderstanding from inside by tracing the flight or thread of empty space running through things, even a relation that's concordant.

Seeds disperse in summer air.

Sunrays cease to represent parallel passages in a book, i.e., not coming from what I see and feel.

Relation is in the middle, relay, flower description *to* flower becoming of my eye between light and heart.

Now, information has released imaginative function from authors.

I send an interrupted line over the top of space, past the middle cinematically, when you can no longer stand what you put up with before.

At night, part of her numbed to pain and part woke to what occurred.

Working backward in sleep, the last thing you numbed to is what wakes you.

What if that image were Eros as words?

I write to you and you feel me.

What would it be like if you contemplated my words and I felt you?

Animals, an owl, frog, open their eyes, and a mirror forms on the ground.

When insight comes in a dream, and events the next day illuminate it, this begins your *streaming* consciousness, synchronicity, asymptotic lines of the flights of concordances.

An owl opens its eyes in deep woods.

For the first time, I write and you don't know me.

Milkweed I touch floats.

2

One can experience another's energy as stress.

At first, I felt attacked by this attribution of the symptoms of my illnesses.

I was frightened thoughts and feelings could be externalized.

Then, I saw sunrise frequencies emanate from your body, like music.

An excited person in light absorbs wavelengths she herself gives off, as if light were the nutrient for feeling.

Color is the mirror where we see ourselves with living things, scarlet neck feathers, infant asleep across your heart, like to like.

Attention gives light: shine on a baby's calf; as he hears what I say, I become that.

Look at my body as light reflecting the thought and feeling, it's not safe to be here.

Remove anxiousness over persons you yearn for, stepping back to observe, like an animal in the fourth dimension.

Since animals don't judge, their evolving cosmic skills are a source of richness for us.

A bird lands on the rim of your tub; a wolf licks your baby's head.

When she cries and the part of you who cries wakes, do you hold her to suppress feeling?

Yearning can't be split and the animal lost, ahead of time.

3

My words unroll a plane of consistence they do not pre-exist—particles, fluxes the colors of spring.

Desire individuates through affects and powers I place on a page or plane of light vibrations, like a flowering field.

His autonomic response is to constrict breath against the feminine, magnetism of gems, consciousness emanating from stars symbiotic with individuation.

When I hear ants are telepathic, I see tiny words trying to communicate.

Then, they file across my clock, it's time to go.

Life manifests everywhere in the cosmos, but as we eliminate species here, we lose access to other realms.

So, discovering a new species is a great event.

Numinousness in the psyche emerges as from morphic fields, our wish for the animal tuning to its light or waveform, like the light of sex.

When you doubt this, you place a piece of "someone" on a pedestal to examine, a gap.

Breathe the shard back into yourself.

In your memory, scarlet feathers of a beloved macaw begin a glow arising from the exact color of connection.

Warmth, which was parallel, moves across the shard, smoothes and makes it porous, matter breath, light materializing ants and words.

Parallel Lines

1

While I questioned my dream, whether or not he was a spirit guide, I closed off imagination not contained in the world.

The dream is a touchstone, face to your face.

In the morning, my husband would no more look for its trace than a fish, who sees water as his palace, sees it flow.

I wake, like a bird among thousands of traces of small birds' passing through the space.

Can you perceive traces, virga, pigment in a substrate of dawn light, as one speaks *yes,* pigment, *no,* substrate, *seeing,* pigment.

Not waking is a substrate, as no love is to love.

So, you go out and meet someone.

Encountering a dream trace by day is face-to-face transmission: *lightning strikes the lamp between us in a summer storm.*

It's pouring water into ocean and spreading it endlessly, dawn commencing on mud walls; lamp shines out.

No trace continues.

It flows, as this summer flows through spring.

Spring flowed through itself, a space, and summer is space I break, pecking from inside my dream and outside, telling it to you.

2

My eye encounters ocean floor, light on sand, horizontal bands of color with no distinction between dream object and heightened sensation—looms of sunrays, rain.

Then, emptiness is earth during the moments of my walk.

When I crossed a ridge into the next arroyo and crossed that, you were present.

Yet presence and today are like snapshots from a pin-hole camera, no substrate.

Spring flows through my walking in autumn.

Not walking is last year to this year, words arriving, mind ancillary to words, as I recall your manner of thinking, of feeling happiness, of walking, looking, of immediately telling your dream.

Pick up a weft line then and thread it here, edge of memory like film exposed beyond an image, sky not hindering white clouds from flying?

So, speaking is not stained by my not hearing.

He's concealed within my not hearing and in his speaking, like not remembering someone whose card I find in my bag, or words in a mother tongue comprehensible to those experiencing words and no words as sky on film.

White clouds are data beneath words in blinding light.

They're not debris in the mind.

3

Where does mist come from on the mountain?

How will dust materialize color in air light moves through in parallel, energized lines, fabric?

Why does one person see time as a sequence of good health, exceptional beauty, a line of luck?

A moment of experience commences a train of causes for all plausible outcomes.

A moment over-exposed on film regains vibrations of a web in rain.

Like a causal succession of blood through the heart, myriad sight-lines construct crimson, then lose brightness in air, if not retained as the present.

Cast oxygen across the lines, a person walking toward a mountain across water routes north to south, z's of run-off, taking the interrupted line (of walker A) across voids.

There are fatigue lines of will struggling, as if flowing water were sand in drought.

Mist is breath not dissipated by space, joy endorphins chasing adrenaline exhaled into sky.

Mist, part of the plane, drifts through planes.

It does not tear time to carry across just a single emotional line of one self in one time, like a wind that comes up.

The lines accentuate each other, land stepped with waves, grass stippled with pines, indigo threads interwoven with exquisite gold strands in the dream palace.

Red Quiet

1

I look into his eyes and feel my awareness expand to contain what he will tell me, as if what he says is a photograph of landscape and in my mind will be a painting of "Hill," "Part of the Cliffs," "Purple Hills."

These words are the opposite of verisimilitude.

Between his location and mine is white space constituting the flow of emotion on which we travel, when moving our awareness of a place to a moment.

Ghost particles exist on a border between something that happens and increasing probability it will happen again.

Words spoken with force gather particles.

A person enters, and now my room is encased in dread.

Even so, I was too concerned, like a young girl trying to understand feelings through my feeling.

If existence is vibration, everything creates sound—trees, heart cells.

A listener, like water, resonates dread in a blue vase, in glasses.

I send out an opposite emotion of warmth, welcome, the way scientists erase sound with sound.

2

When a person enters, space is fragmented.

A red amaryllis in sun quarters the breakfast room.

Each large petal extends a moment vector into space, like the crystalline structure of water freezing, consciousness registering time.

The idea that red as in sex, love, will open the gates of heaven is trying to substitute a feeling of heaven for the experience of heaven.

Red maintains a strong impression of the body, while consciousness flows along inner images.

When an amaryllis bends toward light and I don't turn it, I may still change the feeling of a stalk leaning in my memory, whirling with the sun, crossing from my experience to larger probability.

My love for the blossom partakes of transitions fields create with emotion, I mean certain locations attract events.

So, I object to expending energy trying to alleviate a situation with horticulture.

I look into a blossom, and its image sinks into me like winter rain.

A cause is not determined, when I perceive, with its intense presence, the isolation of the *red* hue, as in *white* space previously mentioned.

3

Our conversation is a wing below my consciousness, like the organization in blowing cloth, eddies of water, its order of light on film with no lens.

A higher resonance of story finds its way to higher organization, like data swirling into group dreams.

Then story surfaces as if recognized; flies buzzing in your room suddenly translate to: "Oh! You're crying!"

So, here I hug the old person, who's not "light" until I embrace him.

My happiness at seeing him, my French suit constitute at the interface of wing and occasion.

Postulate whether the friendship is truly fulfilling.

Reduce by small increments your worry about the nature of compassion or the chill of emotional identification among girlfriends, your wish to be held in the consciousness of another, like a person waiting for you to wake.

Postulate the wave nature of wanting him to wait (white space) and the quanta of fractal conflict, point to point, measuring the outline of a petal, shore from a small boat.

Words spoken with force create particles.

He calls the location of accidents a morphic field; their recurrence is resonance, as of an archetype with the vibration of a seed.

My last thoughts were bitter and helpless.

A friend witnessing grief enters your consciousness, illuminating your form, so quiet comes.

Acknowledgment

Grateful acknowledgment is made to the publishers of my books from which these poems have been selected:

Summits Move with the Tide (The Greenfield Review Press)

Random Possession (I. Reed Books)

The Heat Bird (Burning Deck Press)

Hiddenness (Whitney Museum Library Fellows)

Empathy (Station Hill Press)

Sphericity (Kelsey St. Press)

Endocrinology (U.L.A.E. and Kelsey St. Press)

The Four Year Old Girl (Kelsey St. Press)

Nest (U.L.A.E. and Kelsey St. Press)

Grateful acknowledgment to the editors of the magazines where my new poems first appeared: *The American Poet, Bomb, No Magazine, The Village Voice, Volt,* and to Rutgers Center for Innovative Paper and Print.

Deep gratitude to Barbara Guest for her inspiration and friendship.

Designer: Ralph Fowler

Text: 11.5/15 Granjon

Display: Granjon

Compositor: BookMatters, Berkeley

Printer and binder: Friesens Corporation

51079